AMERICA:

Practical Solutions

For The 21st Century

STEVEN CHARLES

$16 USD

STEVEN GRAHAM CHARLES

STARS IN THE WIND

SOUTH OF BAGHDAD

THE MAN IN BLUE

AMERICA:
Practical Solutions For The 21st Century

DancingGroundEntertainment@gmail.com

FOR
THE
CHILDREN
OF
AMERICA
&
THEIR
PARENTS

<u>ABIDE BY THE PRAGMATIC CHOICE</u>

The future of our country cannot be dictated any longer by partisan politics, money, religion, or racial issues. The future dictates we must adhere to common sense solutions that will work for everyone, not to just a few holding the power to resist change and stymie evolution.

Most of the issues being addressed here are closely related or connected so that is why an A-Z approach to these important subjects has been adopted. You may find some issues and ideas are repeated in more than one chapter simply because one societal problem can directly affect another in a different area. Or a point is merely being sharpened.

Our Founding Fathers, as brave and literate as they probably were, could not be oracles or seers to know what would happen to America and the world 250 years later. Back then they had a small population of 2.5 million, not the 330 million plus we now have in 2021. They only had 13 States, not the 50 States plus dependent territories nowadays.

They didn't really see an end to slavery, nor a brutal and divisive Civil War, nor the powerful industrial manufacturing empire in America. Nor could they see two great World Wars, major conflicts in Korea and Vietnam, Prohibition, the Great Depression, airplanes, trains, automobiles, social advances, movies, atomic bombs, computers, space travel, the internet, lobbyist influence, Political Action Committees, Artificial Intelligence, social networks, nor many more unforeseeable things that have developed.

Most of the issues being addressed here are closely related or connected so that is why an A-Z approach to these important subjects has been adopted. You may find some issues and ideas are repeated in more than one chapter simply because one societal problem can directly affect another in a different area, or a point is merely being sharpened.

Here in the first quarter of the twenty-first century we too do not know what great innovations the human minds of ours and the world society as a whole will ultimately come up with. All we do know is that many new great innovations in many areas will continue to push humanity ahead again in ways we could not now possibly comprehend; and as a society we must be ready to embrace and grow with the innovative progress that is so surely to come.

This is not a forum to mislead with a lot of statistical numbers which can be manipulated about one way or the other, all depending on someone's political perspective. Some numbers come from the Government, or scholars, or researchers like myself.

The people who will argue the most against the judgement and validity of any of these proposals will undoubtedly be those for whom any changes in the status quo will affect them the most. This includes Lawmakers currently on the take, Energy Companies, Special Interest Groups, Political Action Committees, the Prison Industry, Domestic Terrorist Groups, White Supremacists, Federal Judges including the Supreme Court, some Public Service workers, the Executive Branch, and the IRS.

They may argue these ideas and solutions are somehow perhaps radical and not very realistic, since we the people cannot possibly hope to project a common sense approach to solve complex problems which we the commoners are obviously not smart enough to truly understand. We shall see, we shall see.

Almost all of the following issues are normally debated from both extreme ends of the political or cultural spectrum, but the real Practical Solutions, the only ones which will ultimately work for the majority, always exists in a very definitive middle ground.

The ideas and conclusions presented here are based on the overwhelming wealth of statistics and opinions that already do exist, and if you should wish to Google or Wikipedia anything contained herein to either confirm or dispute these Practical Solutions it is most surely your inalienable right to do so.

The people who will argue the most against the judgment and validity of any of these proposals will undoubtedly be those for whom any changes in the status quo will affect them the most. This will include Lawmakers and Politicians currently on the take, Energy Companies, Special Interest Groups, Political Action Committees, the Prison Industry, Domestic Terrorist Groups, Judges on all levels including the Supreme Court, some Public Service workers, perhaps even the Executive Branch, and of course the Internal Revenue Service.

They may all argue these ideas and solutions are perhaps radical and not very realistic, since we the lowly common people cannot possibly hope to project a common sense approach to solve complex problems which we are supposedly not smart or competent enough to truly understand.

We shall see, we shall see.

Most of the following issues discussed here are normally debated from both extreme ends, but the practical solution, the only one which ultimately will work, exists in a truly definitive middle ground which most reasonable Americans welcome.

The ideas and conclusions presented here are based on the overwhelming wealth of statistics and opinions that already do exist, and should one wish to Google or Wikipedia anything contained herein to either confirm or dispute these Practical Solutions, it is your inalienable right to do so.

The most defining issues within have to do with Human Rights pertaining to Foreign, Families, Women, LGBTQ), Military and Foreign Affairs, Immigration, Naturalization, Criminal Justice, National Referendums, Health Care, Congress, Term Limits, Infrastructure, Homelessness, Poverty, Economic Stimulus, Corruption, Extremism, Jobs, and Taxation; among others of National importance.

There are those who somehow believe they are right about everything for everyone, and they may falsely label others as either a radical liberal or an extremist right wing conservative. What is really right for everyone is to follow a pragmatic course that leads right down the middle of the road.

Enjoy the ride wherever it may take you.

Steven Charles

<u>BIRTH CONTROL</u>

THE PROBLEM:
Some believe in the right to abortion, while others do not.

PRACTICAL SOLUTIONS:
One of the most highly contentious, and oftentimes loudly debated issues is the subject of abortion. To those who by their own judgement are the higher ground moral species, meaning the religious and conservative so-called backbone of American society, anything other than a Pro-Life stance on the question of abortion is labeled an absolute sin.

But Pro-Choice must remain a legitimate right and law, because as a nation based on freedom we all have to ultimately support a Woman's Right To Choose what happens to her own body after it is physically infiltrated by a man for any reason.

Abortion though, should never be a government funded method of contraception; except in cases diagnosing severe health problems, rape (including statutory), or incest.

Males must come to the realization they are equally responsible for pregnancies and must be held accountable for any costs involved in an abortion, as the pregnancy would not have occurred without their physical participation.

The biased argument that she really wanted sex or was asking for it won't fly anywhere except in the minds of those men responsible; or the hateful religious extremists who claim they legitimately possess some almighty moral conviction in order to try and enforce any Pro-Life restrictions.

Planned Parenthood should primarily be funded as an educational source for sex education and contraception. Any abortions approved should nomimally be either health, rape, or incest related. Anything else they consider should be privately funded by Pro-Choice supporters, who are many in number. What they do is not subject to the opinion of others. Neither any Governments, nor religious groups, should ever have any moral or legal jurisdiction over what a woman chooses to do with their body.

The bottom line in this discussion is Men in Power have no right at all to dictate what a woman does. After all, through fame, intimidation, threats, celebrity, wealth or power these same men may have caused these oftentimes unwanted pregnancies to happen solely by their own physical actions.

WHO WILL OBJECT:
Religious groups, Conservative zealots.

CAMPAIGN FINANCE REFORM

THE PROBLEM:
American politicians have somehow legitimized the practice of being bribed through campaign finance donations and other gifts in order to facilitate the approval or rejection of laws affecting various special interest groups.

PRACTICAL SOLUTIONS:
Despite the many partisan introduced laws to the contrary, money does not really constitute free speech in any literal sense, but it does currently allow for the legalized bribery and extortion of elected officials.

Under the current system we cannot really trust all of our lawmakers to step up with the necessary integrity and do the right thing by saying no to rich campaign donors, PACs, or Special Interest Groups. From their perspective, otherwise how would they be able to collect the millions of dollars they think they will need to influence voters again and win re-election? Many are currently being enriched by the system in place, and are more than hesitant to promote any meaningful financial change that somehow penalizes them.

Lawmakers and Legislators will never really agree to true Campaign Finance Reform since it affects them directly, so the issue must be decided through a National Referendum to enact a Constitutional Amendment in order to level the election playing field by limiting the amount of hard, soft, and dark money currently being contributed to a candidate or their political party. This will significantly lower the costs of political campaigns by putting an end to the undue influence and sometimes unlimited contributions Political Action Committees and SuperPacs have had in elections.

In the infamous and truly insidious Citizens United case argued before the Supreme Court earlier this century it was somehow ruled that political campaign contributions, just like lobbying, may be interpreted as a means of free speech. If money literally flowed from someone's mouth this might actually be true, but it was an obviously partisan political interpretation of the Constitution which was cheered on by its proponents. To its detractors it was extremely disheartening and a clear indication of how abject political bias on the Supreme Court can affect decisions which are supposedly determined by Constitutional law.

If that incomprehensible decision is not reversed there are still other alternatives to correct the injustice. One is for the Federal Election Commission to put strict and very much lower limits on how much an individual, PAC, or SuperPac can contribute through their so-called "Free Speech". Right now those amounts range anywhere from $2.8K to $106.5K to *Unlimited.* That's right, unlimited cash from dark sources whose donors and interests do not have to be listed. Smells very bad, as foreign entities may be deeply involved.

A much better and honest approach is to limit any contributions from any individual or party or group to $25K and Publicly Fund the rest at an acceptable rate, which many lawmakers who are actually serving in the public interest and not their own personal or special interests, do already support completely. But most of these people are not on the take so what else could be ethically expected of them?

The very wealthy, Political Action Committees and Special Interest Groups, and perhaps even some of the media profiting from the blatantly expensive political advertising system will no doubt object, perhaps most vociferously. They will cry loud and hard about how any changes to the very profitable status quo are not warranted, and somehow infringe upon their supposedly "Free Speech" rights.

But for the intrinsic good of America the issue of Campaign Finance Reform must inevitably come to fruition, and arrive much sooner than later.

WHO WILL OBJECT:

Many members of Congress currently on the take, Special Interest Groups, Political Action and Super Pac groups, and of course the Dark Money Devils who may not even be American.

<u>CONGRESSIONAL MALAISE</u>

THE PROBLEM:

Most Americans do not believe elected officials in Congress are actually doing what they were elected to do.

PRACTICAL SOLUTIONS:

Many Americans who are polled or just discuss the subject among themselves, do not have a very high approval rating of how Congress operates since it is a truly rare occasion when anything meaningful actually gets done for the country due to the ever growing gridlock of partisan politics and the seemingly legalized bribery in play.

Essentially what is wrong with Congress? For many members, unfortunately their actions are motivated more by long-serving party Power Brokers in Congress, and the PACs and Lobbyists funding them; rather than the true "constituents" whose interests they are supposed to be actually representing.

Foremost, America must eliminate the pervasive flow of money from Lobbyists that everyone in the world except some of our ardent Lawmakers see as blatant bribery. Of course, those receiving these funds will all vehemently deny any association with an illegality normally judged a crime in civil and Federal courts, but the money flowing into their campaign or re-election chests clearly proves otherwise.

Congressional control over legislation or actions which are clearly partisan directed must also be reduced. A 60% SuperMajority approval will help eliminate the time currently being wasted on the processing of those initiatives. Currently one political party having a very slight majority of the House or Senate can completely rule out anything that may be important to the slight minority on the other side of the political aisle. So as party majorities in Congress and the Executive Branch can very dramatically change with each election, laws imposed by a previous majority usually go back and forth when another leadership group takes control, with no permanent action ever really being certain except by a Constitutional Amendment.

Congress must also leave expert decisions up to experts in that field, including military expenditures, since no matter what committees any members of Congress sit on or chair, they should never be considered experts in any field unless it was a definitive field of their expertise before they entered Congress. Otherwise, their opinions should be documented as being purely partisan policy related, or perhaps just simply uninformed as most now seem to be.

Our country must endeavor to limit the powers of the Congressional Speakers and Majority leaders from blocking bills and actions from any discussion or votes by the rest of Congress; and institute a more fair SuperMajority approval on discussing or voting on all legislation instead of one party that is having a slim majority being able to completely cancel out the minority. That is not a true Democratic process and the country deserves much better.

This is why a publicly funded true third party system may result in a true coalition government approach where partisan cooperation is the only way to affect change. Those who do nothing to help move important legislation along will undoubtedly be replaced in the next election by those who may pledge to cooperate and actually do so.

Compromise and cooperation after all, are the key ingredients to most relationships; whether personal, business, or legislative.

Term limits will also greatly help do away with the entrenched Power Brokers whose undue influence does not benefit America.

Americans should urge Lawmakers to end the filibuster as it's not a necessary debate and just wastes time; especially when time is of the essence in order to get important problems solved. Filibusters are not needed now, haven't been in the past, nor will they be needed in the future. It has just become a political stunt for one party to delay the actions of another party. Continuing the twisted, corruptible ways in which Congress presently operates is not a Practical Solution for the future of America.

WHO WILL OBJECT:

Some members of Congress, who will be duly noted for their objections and how it stands up to the test of truth.

CONSTITUTION AMENDMENTS

THE PROBLEM:

Some fear Constitutional amendments are neither necessary nor warranted.

PRACTICAL SOLUTIONS:

Purists may cringe at any attempt to amend America's hallowed Constitution, but Amendments to the Constitution have been done at least 25 times before, and history has shown this very necessary refinement to the laws of this country will be exercised many more times again as it helps rectify many important policies our Founding Fathers could not foresee.

America's Founding Fathers had great principles but really had no idea what the future would bring. They created a Democratic society but could not envision the lack of integrity when Lawmakers subverted the principles created.

Several very important Constitutional Amendments are needed. A definite necessity is the long overdue Balanced Budget Amendment which Congress must adhere to in order to reduce the massive Federal Deficit; and put an end to their lust for spending more money than what is available. America, like all its citizens, must learn to live within its means.

A 60% SuperMajority approval is also needed on all Federal legislative bills to promote true bipartisanship action in Congress. A 50.1% majority over a 49.9% minority, usually on strictly partisan political voting is not fair to anyone; especially the American citizens who realize when control of the White House or Congress flips to the other party then past legislation merely gets wiped away, usually solving little in the long run.

Term Limits both for Congress and all Federal Judges, including the Supreme Court, is a worthwhile amendment to help move the country forward and away from the tentacles of long serving Power Brokers in Congress and the Judiciary. Change has always been a fundamentally sound approach to improve any institution, including Congress and the Supreme Court. New minds and new ideas inevitably must replace older precepts in order to move the evolution of society along.

The unnecessary Electoral College must quickly be eliminated out of existence. It has never been what the Founding Fathers meant it to be, and is highly subject to manipulation. The popular vote, as in most elections, must be the final determination of any presidential election.

In order to reduce the gigantic amount of money currently being spent and wasted on political campaigns, all Federal Political Elections should be Publicly Funded in order to not allow the Lobbyists and Political Action Committees to buy elections, or affect any Legislation whatsoever.

The only plausible alternatives to these problems and many others are only through Constitutional Amendments or National Referendums; both of which many members of Congress will most likely disavow because they feel it will limit the power they have so righteously been privately funded to have earned. For the positive future of our country we must do away with intractable thinking, now and forever.

WHO WILL OBJECT:

Any members of Congress who appreciate how things are working in their favor.

CRIMINAL JUSTICE

THE PROBLEM:

America claims to be one of the freest Democratic countries on the planet, yet it incarcerates more of its citizens per capita than any other nation in the world.

PRACTICAL SOLUTIONS:

One of the most important decisions facing our country is Criminal Justice, as it now favors the wealthy and overwhelmingly has discriminated racially. On a per capita basis America now incarcerates more citizens than any other country in the world, including even those many repressive governments run by autocratic dictators. It is a truly shameful moniker for America to have, and certainly no claim to fame.

Those who profit from and vehemently defend the current Criminal Justice system, will claim it is because we are a Law and Order country. Which we are not, as our high crime rates validate the real truth of the matter.

Federal laws must find a way to override all the old and oftentimes blatantly racist State laws for incarcerating prisoners. It should be a crime or censure for any States to impose harsh judgments on non-violent crimes. This can be accomplished either through a reduction in Federal funds, the loss of Federal contracts, or even a Judicial pardon. After all, you can't kill the snakes unless you cut off their heads.

The Cash Bail System must also be eliminated as it is highly discriminatory against those who simply do not have the funds to be released, while those who have the cash or bail collateral are allowed to walk out the jail door no matter what they may have done. But truly violent offenders charged with a felony should not be allowed on the streets no matter how much money they have, as they could well be flight risks or still a danger to others. The rest of those who are non-violent heading towards court should be released on their own recognizance, or home monitored as necessary.

Mandatory minimum sentences for all non-violent crimes and reprehensible third strike laws only benefit the capricious prison system industry and those who profit from it directly at taxpayer expense. Truth be told, these so-called deterrents to crime don't make citizens any safer.

Still, we must enact Federal Maximum Sentences for all violent crimes, but also put an end to Capital Punishment except for cases resulting in convictions of either Domestic or International Terrorism which have caused deaths. Lethal injection executions were a bad mistake from the beginning, still fraught with procedural problems. If someone needs to be executed, a firing squad is really the best way.

There must be an end to the use of private prisons on Federal convictions, which in truth are only more profitable to these private prison companies if more and more people are incarcerated, and at taxpayer expense of course.

America must end all incarceration for drug use alone, or any nonviolent sales or possession convictions. Divert individuals to drug courts and treatment programs; perhaps even in abandoned military facilities which can be converted to treatment centers and cost taxpayers far less than jails and prisons will. Leaving non-violent people in prison is not a form of rehabilitation. It is simply inhumane.

It is extremely essential for the Federal Government to closely control all maximum prison capacities to reduce violence, and eliminate the dire influence correctional officer unions seem to have over incarceration policies. Removing all non-violent inmates will help further this step. Hopefully, voters in many States will urge their legislators to follow this example. If not, the Federal Judiciary can override these policies, as necessary.

An investment must be made into Public Defenders' offices to ensure all defendants really have access to quality legal counsel, perhaps through a pro bono system with local lawyers. Usually the PD office promotes the usual plea bargain procedure which helps the Public Defender to eventually move into the District Attorney's office through their abject cooperation with the DA's prosecutors. Might be good for them, but not entirely so for the client.

The defining problem here, above any and all others, is really how the white majority in this country, of which I am definitely a part of, ultimately uses its legal powers to subject people of other races to penalties they don't often charge those of their own skin color with.

That is not nearly justice, but it should be a crime.

WHO WILL OBJECT:

Private prison companies, corrections officer unions, racists, and proponents of mandatory minimum sentences.

DEMONSTRATIONS

THE PROBLEM:
Peaceful demonstrations can sometimes turn violent, but the violence is not always started by the demonstrators.

PRACTICAL SOLUTIONS:
Peaceful demonstrations are one thing, a proud heritage to American free speech; but violent demonstrations are quite another. America so profoundly witnessed that reality on January 6, 2021 when a lawless mob of anti-Government protesters stormed the halls of Congress to try and circumvent Constitutional law, if not punish any Lawmakers they could eventually get their anarchy fueled, rabid mad-dog hands on.

Some rioters were maybe just diehard supporters of the loser in an election who simply lost their control in the heat of the moment, and at the President's urging; but the ringleaders and provokers have been found to be members of extremist right wing militias who are nothing more than Domestic Terrorists trying to somehow project themselves as "true patriots". Nothing could be further from the truth. They should all be prosecuted to the full extent of the law. It would not be hard for a President to decree that no weapons of any kind are to be allowed near Federal property anywhere at any time. Or brandishing firearms in a public gathering anywhere, in any State, is a violation of Federal law and will be penalized. This would not directly affect anyone's ability to protest peacefully.

Rioters anywhere should be arrested and incarcerated if their supposedly peaceful demonstration of free speech has morphed into something else completely. It really doesn't matter if they are left wing fascism fighters, Black Lives Matter protesters, or right wing white supremacists. What only matters is what they actually do. The use of Homeland Security, the FBI, ATF, the National Guard, and local police to enforce the cessation of violent demonstrators and rioters is not only warranted, but it should actually be expanded. More forcefully if necessary. Looting, setting fires, and assault is not peacefully demonstrating.

Officers on the ground must also be vetted better, especially in terms of racial and extremist views in order to ensure true public service integrity. Law enforcement officers on any level should not be allowed to move aggressively against any one group; while doing little or nothing to another group also engaging in protest, but may be more aligned with their own personal beliefs.

WHO WILL OBJECT:

Some police officers, police unions, and perhaps the ACLU and some other groups.

<u>DISCRIMINATION</u>

THE PROBLEM:

America has one of the world's most diverse ethnic populations, yet discrimination against those of color, gender, or lifestyle continues and has only exacerbated the problem.

PRACTICAL SOLUTIONS:

Unfortunately, there are still people in our country who seem to believe non-whites such as Asians, Hispanics, Muslims, Native Americans, and African Americans do not belong in this country. These bigots believe different races are not subject to the inalienable rights guaranteed by our Constitutional laws. Discrimination based on racism cannot be tolerated in America, which was founded by immigrants from all over the world. Discrimination in all its hateful forms is simply both a tragedy and a crime, and not nearly representative of most Americans or their values.

Criminal liabilities must be expanded to protect all citizens. Discrimination of State, Federal or Constitutional law by any spurilous religious belief must also be eliminated and perhaps even prosecuted. Religious freedom has always amounted to the thinly veiled ability to clearly discriminate against others who are not of their own beliefs, or skin color. Bigotry has no lawful place in America, even in a church.

Reenactment of the Equal Rights Amendment will especially help Women getting equal pay for equal jobs as they so rightfully deserve. It will also help protect the entire growing LGBTQ voters who are discriminated against due to their choice of lifestyle, which really has nothing to do with any of those supposed moralists who adamantly oppose any person's freedom to choose a different lifestyle.

Racial discrimination in all its utterly ugly forms is undoubtedly the most prevalent and ongoing disease in America, and which needs to be eradicated through both education and greater enforcement of laws which are already well established, but are clearly not being enforced enough by those in power who may be discriminatory themselves

Hate crimes must be better addressed not only on a national level, but definitely on a local level as well, as this is where the majority of these abuses occur. Those responsible for violations should be prosecuted to the full extent of the law. Not just locally, but on a Federal level as well.

WHO WILL OBJECT:

Some police officers, most right wing extremist white power groups, and some elected officials as well.

<u>DISEASE CONTROL</u>

THE PROBLEM:

America and the rest of the world are ill-equipped to handle a disease pandemic.

PRACTICAL SOLUTIONS:

In 2021 most Americans could not have expected what the Covid-19 virus pandemic would do to society, both here and in the rest of the world over the difficult past year. Poor leadership, a lack of essential medical equipment, and a painfully slow political acceptance of the actual problem by many influential people only made it far worse.

Today there are still some right wing conspiratorial extremists, obviously not the most intelligent of our citizenry, who loudly claim it wasn't really a pandemic like the Black Plague which wiped out whole countries in Europe. As if over a million plus dead worldwide already isn't enough proof for these fools. In truth folks, vaccines and medical procedures have improved greatly since medieval times.

By the year 2015 the presidential administration had developed in place a critically necessary program and the necessary resources to handle any threats of a potentially pandemic virus threatening America. It wasn't a matter of "If It Would Happen", it was merely just a question of "When".

The completely inexperienced incoming president in 2016, decided to eliminate that failsafe program as being unnecessary; for no other seeming reason except the economic power he had could be wielded to do just that. Any savings could ostensibly be transferred to other pet projects the President deemed more important than impending disaster.

In early 2020 when the pandemic first hit, America was totally unprepared to deal with the vast consequences which resulted. There was a clear leadership void, not only in the Executive Branch, but also in Congress as a whole. Since pandemic healthcare resources had been eliminated, the country could not respond quickly or effectively to this crisis. Many died unnecessarily from a very painful and callous Presidential decision. A year later in 2021 we are looking at over 600,000 deaths in America alone, of which it has been scientifically documented that at least 50% of those fatalities could have been prevented if the necessary tools and leadership skills were in place. Unfortunately they were not.

The per capita death rate in America is among the highest reported of anywhere in the world. It should never have been this way. The blame clearly falls on Government officials at all levels whose partisan political buffoonery negated proper public health initiatives.

Effective vaccines are now becoming widely available and eventually the current virus pandemic will hopefully be controlled enough to help make most lives around the world return to some substance of normality. There will still be some individuals who will refuse to take the vaccine due to religious or conspiratorial beliefs. Any contact with these potentially contagious fools should be avoided by all.

Our country, along with the rest of the world, must be better prepared in the future to address environmental changes, diseases, and calamities we cannot foresee but will ultimately must face, especially with climate change. As polar icecaps and glaciers continue to melt and potentially expose dangerous latent bacteria, the world will undoubtedly face even more deadly diseases in the future. We must be prepared and willing to face those threats by supporting the scientific leaders who are dedicated to helping us survive.

In America we must make sure no one, not even a sitting President, can ever unitarially control public health issues in this country. Politicians and elected officials are not doctors, disease experts, or for the most part not even scientifically oriented in any way. Oftentimes, while they may have won an election, their lack of expertise in many important areas must be controlled by a Congressional SuperMajority or better yet a Constitutional Amendment to insure the safety of the country, no matter who is the elected leader.

WHO WILL OBJECT:
Any fools who can't or won't accept reality.

<u>DOMESTIC TERRORISM</u>

THE PROBLEM:

White supremacist groups seek to promote anarchy against anyone who does not support their extremist beliefs.

PRACTICAL SOLUTIONS:

It is in the absolute best interests of all Americans to demand Law Enforcement to aggressively go after all Violent Street Gangs, White Supremacist Groups, and any Foreign Terrorist Cells operating in America. People may think China or Russia or Iran are the biggest threats to our country, but the truth of the matter strikes closer right here at home.

This is what the FBI and Homeland Security should focus on, instead of hunting for illegal immigrants who haven't committed violent crimes, and who are not nearly as dangerous as some of the born and bred citizens of ours already here.

Right wing militias have views toward overthrowing the government and waging civil war against people of other races and political persuasions. These disturbed minds try to portray themselves as patriots, but in reality are just enemies.

Very alarming is that some current or former Law Enforcement officers and military veterans share these same twisted views and can actually stand in the way of, or look the other way from, dealing with their own brethren rats in our society. So who then can we really trust?

If enough angry but probably not too intelligent zealots are sent to prison for twenty or so no parole years on Domestic Terrorist charges, perhaps their hateful recruitment base may think twice about joining the cause.

Street Gangs in America are also a growing problem as we continue to seemingly allow Central American youth gangs to operate freely within our borders. We could incarcerate or deport any of them as Domestic Terrorists if the resolve to do so is really there. Of additional concern is the many foreign nationals who come to America on visas and then stay here by disappearing into ethnic neighborhoods, perhaps buying false identification in the process. Depending on beliefs they could be part of foreign Domestic Terrorist cells. Our visa system needs upgrading as it is presently a liability to our security.

These angry, disillusioned fools all conveniently see themselves as true saviors of this or another country, but in truth they are just violently criminal insurrectionists falling in line with some of our country's greatest enemies, now and throughout history. Put them in prison, perhaps in Guantanamo Bay with other terrorists, or wipe them out by force if needed should they attempt to incite violence in the future.

A good and deserving lesson for truly fake patriots would be to revoke their citizenship and ship the whole lot of them off to truly autocratic countries like Russia, North Korea, China, or Iran; where the same destructive anti-American hatred and beliefs may be shared. Hitler would have loved these psychos. America definitely does not.

WHO WILL OBJECT:
Right wing white supremacists and their followers. Plus any foreign national cells plotting terrorism.

ECONOMIC STIMULUS

THE PROBLEM:

A pandemic ravaged society needs much more massive economic stimulus until it can right itself again.

PRACTICAL SOLUTIONS:

Here in 2021 we are still in the hopefully waning but still deadly stages of a global pandemic which has caused great harm to our country, since most people haven't been able to even work or play together safely anymore.

Some people in Government and Congress are still being paid nonetheless while many in the mainstream are now unemployed; but many have slowly but surely seen the need for stimulus payments to those in society who need it the most. Other lawmakers, who maybe aren't financially hurting themselves, may not see it as being all that necessary.

Let's start with Seniors, many of whom receive Social Security checks that still keep most of them way below the Federal Poverty Limit. What will they do with any stimulus money? They will buy things they really need. When it is safe they might be able to travel and visit others in their family who love them. Good for their hearts, but also a great benefit for the economy as a whole. America must fund all Seniors on Social Security, many of whom may be our grandparents, at or above the Federal

Poverty Levels. That would be true Economic Stimulus for those needing it the most.

America should also drastically reduce or even eliminate Student Loan debt which will save up to 50 million Americans from $200 to $300 a month in payments. Where will they spend their savings? On the economy of course.

Removing many politically instituted import tariffs and most agricultural subsidies will also greatly help the economy. America can become a manufacturing giant again by helping fund the evolution of our industrial infrastructure by not rewarding companies who send jobs away outside our borders. Again, this also creates Economic Stimulus.

A Balanced Budget Amendment and a Presidential Line Item Veto is necessary to direct expenditures to our infrastructure projects and the massive jobs potential it will create. Extremely low unemployment rates resulting from new job initiatives will also help to reduce homelessness, crime, and a host of other disturbing social problems.

Funding more pre and post school day care will help families trying to make ends meet. Economic Stimulus again.

Our country cannot keep paying out what it doesn't really have by just borrowing more money. When a country is over six trillion dollars in debt and pays out the most interest on those loans to an economic rival like China, this formula is not financially sustainable. Debt is continually growing and proponents of increasing it claim the interest rate isn't all that expensive. Really? The reality is, sooner or later debts will have to be paid, which leaves future generations a massive Federal debt they did not incur, but must find ways to pay off.

There is a debate over which political party actually contributes more to America's Gross Domestic Product (GDP) output. Republicans, who float tax cuts as a way to help the people; usually construct these to help their richest donors more than the lower or middle classes which need it the most. Yet they market their tax reductions as the poorer being the prime beneficiary of their generous actions. Sadly, the patently naive electorate actually believes it must be true.

In the last 80 years of our history, going back to Franklin D. Roosevelt, economists have clearly determined that Democratic administrations have outperformed their Republican counterparts on the GDP by almost 2.5 to 1. Roosevelt of course, was at the top; and the infamous #45 was way at the bottom, even with all his lame excuses included. The truth is he was at the bottom every year of his four year run, not in just the last viral year of his inglorious reign.

WHO WILL OBJECT:

Economists and conservative politicians who selfishly claim no more "handouts" are needed. We'll get to those handouts later.

<u>EDUCATION</u>

THE PROBLEM:

America's educational system does not adequately prepare students for the paths in society that lie ahead.

PRACTICAL SOLUTIONS:

It is amazing how much the Department of Education spends and how little the country actually has to show for it. The Education Secretary is politically appointed to a Cabinet position with a huge budget, usually as a political favor to a financial contributor. Often they are unqualified bureaucrats.

From a truly political appointee standpoint we might get someone without educational credentials who is just being the mouthpiece for a political party. Or we might get someone injecting a new curriculum and the resulting bureaucratic initiatives which are confusing or not financially supported.

What can the Department of Education still be good for? At the highest level of education, to provide tuition free public college tuition for those with low household incomes, or those who serve at least two years in public service or the military. Give them a chance to better themselves in return for what they have paid forward in the service to our country. 2 years for an AA degree, or 4 years for a Bachelor's degree.

Student loans must be allowed to be relieved through bankruptcy, just like any other debt. Reducing or eliminating them is an even better idea. The bill is now $1.6 trillion with borrowers still owing at least $30K each.

Children and their parents are taught to believe they must go into huge personal debt if they want to be educated for a college degree which may possibly provide them with a higher expected income during their adult life. Definitely not always the case as many graduates go into the workforce with no job offers, but still a hundred thousand or more dollars in Student Loans they are legally required to pay back. It sure doesn't sound like a very good deal from their standpoint.

The Student Loan Program is essentially a colossal scam. College costs continue to rise, over 200% in the past 20 years, while the average wages for graduates don't even come anywhere close to that. Colleges and universities say these necessary increases pay for improvements, which are mostly country club/spa in actuality and have nothing really to do with education. It also pays for the ever increasing athletic coaches and faculty raises. With private universities it is up to families or a scholarship to fund attendance, but for State funded colleges this should not be part of their operating criteria.

Unless someone wants to be a doctor, lawyer, scientist, or other professional; and unless you or your parents can really afford it, there are much better options than paying the rest of your life for expensive college educations with no guarantees. Students can take courses at Community College for a couple of years then transfer to a State College. If anything is owed it will be manageable. Or go online and do it cheaper and easier, while working a job or managing a young family.

What should a less powerful Department of Education do? Expand the use of charter schools as they are oftentimes more effective than over bureaucratized and much more dangerous public school systems. Expand all school desegregation allowances. Close old or unsafe schools, rebuild them, or return the property to community programs. Fund three and four year old preschool and afterschool coverage to help lower income families have a better life potential.

Instead of property taxes institute a small State or local sales tax which will fund all new or existing programs and benefit everyone involved. Not only just homeowners would be contributing to school funding, but then everyone, including renters, would contribute their fair share.

Teachers could actually get paid what they deserve under a fundamentally new approach. States must dramatically increase teacher salaries in order to retain them as they are far more important assets to the educational system than any of the bureaucrats who continually devalue the importance of educators by not paying them well.

Expanding the use of online learning programs, especially in rural communities and areas where there have been ecological disasters, requires only a computer and internet access which schools will have an overflow of when in-person schooling resumes. The pandemic has shown that while online learning programs may not be the best answer for teaching, it can also be a safe bridge for learning. Would some inner-city students be safer learning from home than in schools and that are obviously not safe for them to attend? Most probably.

High School curriculum must be refocused in order to teach the needed skills future employers want young trainees to have, but which they aren't now getting. Whether in Trades, Law Enforcement, Teaching, Business, Healthcare, or IT more needs to be taught at any earlier age. Vocational programs should be expanded, not eliminated. Not everyone wants a college degree. Many young people just want a good job.

The 2019 rollback of rights for student sexual assault survivors must be rescinded. Colleges must be restricted from forcing students to allow unqualified institutions to investigate or rule on merits or penalties of any physical student assaults. Better it is left up to real law enforcement professionals and not activists hoping to try and weaken the current system further to help young males who may have been implicated for what they consider to be harmless sexual encounters. The victims of such behavior usually feel otherwise.

There is not a true defining need for a huge Federal Department of Education, it's Secretary, or the bureaucracy. Over 15% of the Federal Budget is currently geared toward Education, continually rewarding the country with lackluster results. Eliminating ineffective and unnecessary programs will improve the Department and lower outlays by at least 20%.

The Department of Education should focus efforts on school meal programs, school safety, special education, psychological and mental health counseling, improving schools at every level for Native Americans, and contributing to extended pre-school and after-school funding.

Getting rid of Pell Grants, the Student Loan Program, and other compliances puts the responsibility to improving education back into the hands of State and Local governments. State and Local School Boards must endeavor to control the cost of their bureaucracies governing schools, must campaign to raise teacher's pay significantly, and make certain educators are in control of schools, and not politicians.

WHO WILL OBJECT:

School boards, teacher's unions, and Department of Education employees. Parents, Students, and Teachers will not object much.

<u>ELECTION SANITY</u>

THE PROBLEM:

Political Parties are trying to change election laws when they lose any elections or positions of power.

PRACTICAL SOLUTIONS:

Lately, the focus on elections has been on the alleged expansion of fraudulent practices. A certain politician goes into an election claiming to his rabid followers that the only way this candidate could possibly lose is if the other side cheats. Some supporters actually believe it to be true.

The candidate loses, supporters then loudly cry foul, and many lawsuits and court challenges ensue. Yet there is no evidence from anyone, even in their own party, that any measure of fraud has ever existed. It is simply supposition. But the rabid die-hard followers still choose to believe it is true, because this is what the candidate preached to them. Would the candidate actually be lying to them? Politicians?

What is clear is that one party believes only the other party has cheated during an election, but not anyone in their own party of course. But consider this: In that same election the incumbent President goes into the election with an approval rating of only 35%, yet still receives 47% of the vote. It makes you wonder about who in reality was actually doing any cheating. Maybe they just didn't do it enough.

Still, this sore loser implores his avidly extremist supporters to go to Washington on a certain fateful day and storm Congress to try and change legitimate election results. This is the first time in American history where verified election results have been violently disputed by a dangerous insurrection at the urging of an incumbent yet soundly defeated President. These traitors who have attempted this malicious action should either be incarcerated, or as enemies of the country even shot dead should they ever try it again.

So how can we both defend our election processes? Principally by the end to all the outside money donations being injected into elections. There is a great need to have only publicly funded major political parties.

The end of the Electoral College system is also very important for the preservation of the popular vote winner being the true election winner. A SCOTUS decision that Electoral College delegates do not necessarily have to vote along with what their States decided is also extremely troubling. If a system can easily be manipulated then it should be eliminated.

Some very relevant Supreme Court decisions will also help clear the air regarding the integrity of our election process, that is if they are not partisan politics at its worst. SCOTUS should rule that all Federal Election mandates are controlled at the Federal level, while all State and Local elections are validated under State laws and control. This might mean there might be two separate ballots in a Federal

Election year, one under Federal guidelines for Presidential and Congressional races, and the other under any divergent State guidelines.

Once the Electoral College is eliminated, who has the most votes in any state really won't matter as the National popular vote is the true final indicator of Federal Election results. The results then cannot be challenged by any other States or political parties without clear evidence of any ballot or rules tampering. Any of these already discredited suits by parties who lost an election can be labeled as frivolous and subject to censure. Any voter suppression efforts in a State during a Federal election would thus be completely eliminated.

There should be serious consideration given to expanding early voting to at least a month before an election to allow for health protocols and weather problems. Also, making mail-in or absentee ballots due at local election headquarters 15-30 days before election day will give more time for proper certification of these votes, and perhaps even silence the usual naysayers a bit. The votes could actually be counted as they arrive, as long as no totals are released until the end of election day. America must explore any safe and encrypted possibilities of online voting for registered voters only. Detractors will claim this process could be hacked and manipulated, just as they do with all voting tabulation procedures anyway.

One final act imperative to avoiding voter suppression tactics is to restore The Voter

Rights Act, which could also be a great Constitutional Amendment.

WHO WILL OBJECT:

Some election losers and their proponents who are trying to restrict voting options for political purposes.

THE ELECTORAL COLLEGE

THE PROBLEM:
Why is this antiquated institution still allowed to circumvent the popular vote used in all other elections?

PRACTICAL SOLUTIONS:
It's been stated before but bears repeating. In no way, shape, or form does the outdated and totally unnecessary Electoral College operate as it was originally intended by our Founding Fathers. They did not have 50 states to deal with, nor could they envision the angry and divisive partisanship currently gripping our country early in the 21st century. The Electoral College concept would also be totally obsolete in a true multi-party system, which is what America desperately needs to help eliminate partisan gridlock.

The Electoral College is clearly unfair to the popular vote which is the true will of the people, and its rules can be subject to manipulation on many fronts. The winner of the presidential election should be determined by the popular vote only. Period. The only present need for the Electoral College is to swiftly get rid of it, as in forever.

No other country in the world uses such an archaic system as they know it can be easily manipulated to distort election results. Electorate members do not actually even have to vote for what their States decided, which is inherently dangerous.

With no useless Electoral College in effect it means State political delegates are not necessary, and a better third party system can lead to the same coalition government which most democratic countries around the world incorporate. In a true multi-party election no one candidate would probably receive the required 270 electoral votes currently necessary in the Electoral College, so its usefulness is a moot point. The good news is the candidate with the most popular votes would still be the winner in a federal election.

Much of the problem has been in how the States now allocate their Electoral votes. All but a few States have a winner-take-all system in place which gives all the votes in their State to one candidate even if they win that State by just a few votes. Is that fair? No, it is patently ridiculous. If Electoral votes were allocated based on the percentage of actual votes a candidate receives, then that would truly be fair. Based on a fair formula, just by the popular vote the last five presidents elected to office would have been Bill Clinton, Al Gore, Barack Obama, Hillary Clinton, and Joe Biden.

Certainly not everyone will like to acknowledge this truth, but it is definitely real and cannot be ignored.

WHO WILL OBJECT:
State and Congressional lawmakers, especially on the Republican side.

ENVIRONMENTAL REALITY

THE PROBLEM:
Many politicians and special interest groups fail to accept the reality of oncoming ecological disasters.

PRACTICAL SOLUTIONS:
There are still some not-so-bright political minds in our country who choose to not accept the overwhelming evidence and reality of climate change. Greenhouse gas carbon emissions continue to rise, icebergs are melting, the ocean is creeping in closer, temperatures soar to new highs and lows, forests burn more than ever, and both droughts and storms have gotten even worse.

So who do we really believe? Who exactly are these people trying to convince their supporters climate change is merely just a hoax? Do they not believe in scientific data? Do they have a financial interest in the fossil fuel industry? Are they worried about land devaluations along our coasts affecting them before everyone sees the oceans are moving in really fast on our coastlines? Or does the recent relaxation in EPA regulations benefit their businesses? Be the judge.

Whatever is believed for whatever reasons, it is definitely not the reality at hand. Scientific projections show when polar icecaps and glaciers finally dissolve, the world as we know it will forever change. Most coastal cities will be inundated by water or even immersed, not only in America but all over the world. If you don't believe in science you may be able to find some very cheap coastal property in the near future. Maybe even make it your own island! It might not happen in some of our lifetimes, but for our children it will unless steps to suppress these effects are instituted now.

Environmental Protection laws must be expanded, not reduced. America is one the biggest polluters in the world, and must lead the climate change fight by example. Ensuring we achieve a 100% clean energy economy and net-zero emissions no later than 2030 should be a goal. We must remove all reliance on fossil fuels by converting energy needs, including our dilapidated national energy grid, to promote sustainable sources such as solar, wind, and the growing importance of modern battery technology.

The government must mandate that all new vehicles produced or sold in America must be electric or a hybrid. Vehicle manufacturers have already determined gasoline engines are a thing of the past, not the wave of the future.

WHO WILL OBJECT:

Those making money off the system in place, and naysayers avoiding reality until the tide finally washes them out to sea.

HELPING FAMILIES

THE PROBLEM:

American families need help to prosper.

PRACTICAL SOLUTIONS:

Families have been and will always be the inherent strength of not only America but the entire civilization of the world. It is the one true place where love can nurture, grow, and be embraced by all who feel it.

There is so much more America can still do for its families to help keep them together, and much of what can be done is actually based on the success some European countries have established with many similar programs.

There continues to be a great, growing need for more low income housing, both for families and Seniors. Big expensive houses never guarantee happiness within those walls, just bigger bills to pay. Whether HUD is subsidizing the development or it is being built by non-profit groups, smaller all-electric housing is a definite necessity.

In urban environments or small rural communities the land necessary is already there to redevelop abandoned or unsafe buildings which can be torn down and replaced by modern new dwellings. The job creation benefits involved will not only help fuel the local economy, but also attract businesses to a redeveloped and regenerated area where their employees can actually afford to live.

Families should be receiving for pre and post birth of a baby a 16 week paid family leave, even if it is instituted at unemployment rates, although some progressive companies may choose to help subsidize that amount even further. In any event their jobs should by law be waiting for them when they return. Let us all please live by the Golden Rule.

A four week a year paid vacation helps families recharge their lives, and European countries have indeed found happy workers tend to be more productive and loyal to the company when they return from rest or an adventure.

The need for Pre and Post Childcare for ages 3 and up (or when the child is potty trained) has been addressed elsewhere, but the bottom line is families desperately need this. Paying a very small sales tax increase will clearly negate what private pre-school and after school babysitting costs ever amount to. Too often it almost takes up an entire paycheck, so what incentive is there to even go to work?

Finally, an expansion of family counseling programs, even if it is principally done online by video chat, will help families deal with the varied crises most everyone will inevitably face; not just with their children but also with their marriages. Over half of American marriages end in divorce and with children involved they will probably need someone else to talk to, other than warring parents who may confuse them with drastically different views of the situation.

The mental health degradation of children impacted by the actions of their parents and other facets of society cannot be overlooked. Many of us have already been there. Some of us may have found a way to survive through it, but we also probably know of more than a few who did not.

WHO WILL OBJECT:

To make families stronger? Few, if any we should hope.

<u>THE FEDERAL GOVERNMENT</u>

THE PROBLEM:
The disjointed Federal bureaucracy must be reduced and refined to meet the true needs of America.

PRACTICAL SOLUTIONS:
There are many who believe the role of the Federal Government in its citizens' lives should be expanded, while many others say the exact opposite. The real truth, as usual, always lies somewhere in the middle.

Reducing the size of the Federal Government is a long overdue imperative and should be a priority. Many overlapping or truly unnecessary departments can either be consolidated or eliminated, thereby lowering Government expenses and helping reduce the Federal Deficit by trimming the severely bloated bureaucracy currently in place.

Why hasn't it been done before? Principally because those who are essentially controlling the financial waste and bureaucracy are also those who are the most responsible for it, meaning of course Congress. Plus, some Reducing the Federal workforce can easily and relatively painlessly be accomplished just through hiring freezes and/or early retirement. Approximately 6% leave the Federal workforce each year, which would mean a 20-25% force reduction over 4 years. Departments could then reorganize for efficiency and economics.

So what departments and programs does America essentially need? Obviously the Department of Defense, the Military, Congress, Executive Branch, DOJ, Supreme Court, INS, ICE, Treasury/IRS, Federal Courts, State Department, EPA, FDA, Corrections, Homeland Security, FBI, ATF, DEA, CIA, Energy, NASA, Transportation, Education, and Energy, and Native American Affairs (read on further).

The reality is that all of these Departments can be streamlined in a way which reduces expenses and improves productivity. A lot of the intrinsic problems are the archaic ways in which these Federal Departments are forced to go about their business, which is in no way how successful businesses are actually run. But this is how the Federal Government should be run and administered, because it is a business, and unfortunately it is one which continues losing lots of taxpayer money it doesn't actually have to spend.

There is concern that Public Service pensions are already underfunded and that a smarter Federal Government would take into account converting these programs into Social Security benefits as a part of that pension, as well as Medicare in lieu of more expensive healthcare programs being utilized by some early retirees.

This should apply to all members of Congress. Placing Government employees, Congress, and the Military into an expanded

Medicare system strengthens its capabilities and benefits for everyone.

All the rest of these expensive Federal Departments could actually be better handled by each State. Take Agriculture as an example: Each State may have different crop emphasises, and therefore each State is better served by being able to handle their own problems. The same also applies to Commerce, Labor, Interior, Land Management, and any other present duplicate, overlapping or competing agencies. Turn over more power to the States and let them run their own programs as they determine.

Washington should not be an expensive and wasteful welfare society employing civil servants to work in some largely bureaucratic programs which in fact are really and truly unnecessary to the well-being of the nation.

Please go online and look up all the departments and programs you have probably never heard of; which annually waste millions, perhaps even billions of dollars in taxpayer money. The length and breadth of this list is truly frightening. All need to be eliminated as little or any of it will ever be missed, except perhaps for those involved in that particular department. In actuality it is just more of our collective money being wasted.

WHO WILL OBJECT:

Probably some Federal employees and members of Congress, and maybe even the President. So what?

FOREIGN AFFAIRS

THE PROBLEM:
America's handling of Foreign Affairs has left a lot to be desired for a very long time.

PRACTICAL SOLUTIONS:
The ongoing American policy of Foreign Affairs has sometimes been reflected as a politically colonizing aspect directly aligned to the British Empire's failure to ever achieve the same hopeful results. It simply winds up being a loss of lives, money, equipment, prestige, and many other resources. But like the British, we always continue to fail in countries we do not truly understand, or actually even belong in.

As a country we must endeavor to stay out of other countries' conflicts unless it directly threatens our country or our allies. We cannot continue to believe we can solve regional religious or political differences which have seemingly existed forever. Many countries could care less about being a democracy, and we will never change their perception no matter what. History bears out that proof.

Take Afghanistan as a definite example. Billions and perhaps trillions of dollars spent over two decades. What did it accomplish? Did we eradicate the opium fields the Taliban profits from to benefit their operations? No. Have we made the country safer or freer? No. So, in the last twenty years have we accomplished anything meaningful there? No. How about

Iraq? After twenty years have we uncovered any of the Weapons of Mass Destruction that our warhawks falsely gave as the reason for invading there in the first place? No.

Anywhere our military goes uninvited it turns out the same, yet some politicians and defense hawks claim the money and loss of lives was necessary to help promote democracy in places it was clearly not welcomed.

We shouldn't continue to throw money and weapons around at countries which exhibit obvious human rights issues. It makes no sense whatsoever. Helping only our allies does not make us isolationists in any way. It does make us smart and fiscally conservative. Any help provided to non-ally countries should be on a strictly humanitarian basis and nothing more.

If the United Nations or NATO sanctions military action against any country or region then that should be the only way we ever respond militarily to any potential conflict not directly threatening our country.

Foreign Trade deficits must also be addressed as they continue to grow. Our biggest deficit is with China and the bulk of it is actually technological goods which could be manufactured in America, and the cost disparity could be leveled by tax breaks to encourage American companies to build products here. Higher duty taxes on those goods being imported is not the answer as they are not paid by other countries, but instead by American importers who pass the additional costs on to consumers, which results in inflation..

We also run a large trade deficit with Mexico, for many items which could just as easily be manufactured here. Sending lots of jobs to Mexico unfortunately has not resulted in lowering any crime rates or drug cartel control there, so again, tax breaks to produce domestically is the best course of action. Trading with our northern partner Canada is simply good business for both countries, and more free trade should be encouraged.

WHO WILL OBJECT:

The CIA, State Department, some Ambassadors, and a few countries we really don't need to do business with.

<u>GUN CONTROL</u>

THE PROBLEM:

Gun violence and mass shootings continue to plague America at an ever alarming rate. How can it be controlled without endangering Second Amendment rights?

PRACTICAL SOLUTIONS:

It is estimated there are more guns in America than people. It is not really surprising, as the Second Amendment ensures. Gun owners support the belief no attempt should ever be made to try and take away guns from legal owners; and whether you are a gun owner or not, this is a right which must be defended. People fear the Government will try to take their guns away, but even the Government realizes gun seizures are basically unenforceable.

But the right to own weapons should not include the ability to brandish firearms in public to intimidate other groups or citizens during what are supposedly peaceful demonstrations, during elections, or at public gatherings. A Federal Public Firearms Ban during these situations is necessary as there is no conceivable need to brandish weapons if the intent of those holding them are legitimately peaceful. Otherwise, it can lead to greater trouble.

Enhanced Gun Registration Procedures should be implemented to help keep weapons out of the hands of unstable individuals and those belonging to Domestic Terrorist groups.

There should be an AR-15 rifle ban since it is not really a true self-defense weapon. Shotguns and pistols are best for that. AR-15 rifles are not nearly the best hunting rifles available, as their proponents may suggest, so that argument should also be discounted. There is also not a legitimate need for high capacity magazines unless someone is planning to go to war. These weapons are modeled after military rifles whose sole purpose is to kill other people. They should be banned from further public sales and legally confiscated if brandished in public.

If some nut bent on the destruction of themself or others goes into a school or business and fires a gun, it is only because society has given them access to the weapons. Toting your gun around to defend against this never stops it.

One ridiculous provision of gun control being introduced in some States is to force citizens to be licensed to buy ammunition, whether intended for personal defense or sport. This will do nothing to decrease further violence.

Is the author a gun owner? Yes, but only as a defense to those of ill will who are out there.

Otherwise, happy hunting people.

WHO WILL OBJECT:

Probably some of those three letter gun associations, AR-15 manufacturers, criminals, psychos, etc.

<u>HEALTHCARE</u>

THE PROBLEM:

Steps to lower America's exploding healthcare costs have improved, but are not nearly comprehensive enough.

PRACTICAL SOLUTIONS:

The United States has by far the most expensive health care system in the world and despite what politicians and special interest groups loudly claim, it is not nearly the best available anywhere. Back in the day, doctors were not expensive and hospitals were nonprofits run by churches and charities. But corporations and healthcare insurers saw a goldmine to exploit, and exploit it they did.

There are several key ways to dramatically lower our nation's health costs, which now amount to roughly 25% of our country's total expenditures. It could easily be reduced to less than 20% with some very necessary policy changes.

One salient way is the expansion of both Medicare & Medicaid. No, it is not meant to provide Health Care For All, but only for those who truly want and need it. It will certainly be cheaper than any private insurance alternatives.

If any politician in the past few years possessed a better alternative to the Affordable Care Act they never revealed it because they never really had one, and were just spouting off as most politicians tend to do. Since the public at large was already happy with most of the program, it turned out to not be a viable political platform unless someone really had a better plan to offer. Politicians with financial ties to health and companies or their lobbyists labeled the ACA an utter and complete disaster, not really as much for the program itself but for their own reduced financial benefits if they did not bring the program down for their benefactors. The only true disaster would be to allow the Healthcare system to morph back into the more expensive and far less reliable days of old.

The fear mongers in our country claim the Affordable Care Act amounts to socialized medicine, and that this will inevitably lead to more socialist programs in our country. Fortunately, countries around the world which have opted for some sort of socialized medicine to control healthcare costs have reported no evidence of this leading in any way, shape, or form to a more socialist driven society. Fear mongers are not normally identified for spewing anywhere near the truth.

Another way to lower healthcare costs is to extend Medicare to all Federal Government employees, the Military and their families, and Veterans not getting reliable help. This would force Congress to support and extend benefits.

Providing Direct Care for the prevention of illness is also a new tool. Many primary care doctors have chosen to no longer accept any form of health insurance due to the unruly process of actually getting compensated.

Instead, Direct Care doctors charge patients approximately $500 yearly or $50 monthly to provide quarterly check-ups with blood tests included to diagnose any potential health problems before they actually become critical. In a new proposal Preventive Direct Care would be an important part of this program.

Medicare must also revamp its outdated policies to pay only by diagnosis rather than on a procedure by procedure basis hospitals and healthcare providers will exploit every chance they get. Seniors do not always get better from all these supposedly necessary tests given them to up their final bills.

Prescription drug prices are also an area of concern. People rant and rave about Big Pharma and how we have the highest drug prices in the world while most of these drugs are being manufactured very cheaply overseas by these same companies. Everyone has to realize these big companies need all that cash to keep legislators in line and also pay for all their expensive advertising. Could Medicare save a lot by buying directly from Canada or other countries? Sure. But legislators lining their pockets will stifle progress in this regard.

All typical surgical procedures covered under Medicare or Medicaid must be transferred to Ambulatory Surgical Centers, where rates are approximately 50% less than what hospitals charge. Procedures would include normal and c-section births, appendectomies, cataracts, knee and hip replacements, by-pass, angioplasty, and more. This would generate great savings toward the cost of healthcare, but similar procedures in other countries will still cost half as much.

Health Insurance companies being the middleman for healthcare costs and procedure approvals is the main reason almost no other countries allow it. However, Private Health Insurance should remain an option for those who can afford it.

It should be noted that huge medical bills currently account for the vast majority of bankruptcies in our country. People should not have to lose everything they own just to stay healthy or alive. Never was part of the Hippocratic oath.

WHO WILL OBJECT:

Health Insurers, Hospitals, and maybe some Doctors. Families, Patients, and Seniors not so much.

HOUSING & URBAN DEVELOPMENT

THE PROBLEM:

The lack of truly affordable housing contributes to poverty and many other grave social concerns.

PRACTICAL SOLUTIONS:

Companies in high tech, high rent areas complain they are losing employees due to the related cost to live there, and the financial stress it evokes on the employees and their families. Studies show this financial stress directly affects job performance. Yet most companies do not step forward to alleviate a situation which could eventually benefit them.

Large companies should be encouraged to develop more low cost housing options for their employees. Usable land nearby their plants can be utilized and HUD should contribute its help. Progressive benefits like these encourage employees to keep their jobs longer, which businesses want since re-training employees is inherently costly.

In urban areas there may be unused warehouses and abandoned buildings which could be replaced with attractive low income housing. This would not attract local residents, and many other services or related businesses as well.

Housing prices in America continue to soar as building materials continue to rise, especially in areas where there are well-paying jobs. If workers had access to more low cost housing their lives would undoubtedly be enriched.

WHO WILL OBJECT:

Civic bureaucrats, private developers, corporations.

HOMELESSNESS

THE PROBLEM: Homelessness in America continues to grow at an alarming rate.

PRACTICAL SOLUTIONS: One factor in the growth of homelessness is surely the lack of affordable housing available. Another is job loss due to the closure of many businesses during the pandemic.

Another cause is evictions coming from landlords who may see it as an opportunity to raise rents on future tenants. This tactic must be discouraged by fines which would be high enough to make those potential rent increases unprofitable to these landlords. Some really don't care who they put out on the streets, or they wouldn't actually do it. Governments on the Federal, State, and Local levels can take steps to stop this but have not always been successful.

Yet another important consideration is the actual lack of social services being financed to offer mental health help and drug treatment centers to those in need.

But the main cause is actually politics and the lack of action not being taken by civic leaders to cohesively address the problem and offer any viable alternative solutions. Yes, it costs money to provide meals, housing, help, and care for any unfortunate citizens. But the alternatives are completely unacceptable.

Allowing tent cities on sidewalks, in public parks, and abandoned lots is not the answer to the problem. Someone being paid by taxpayers will have to clean up the human waste accumulating, clear up the accompanying rodent infestation, or deal with responding to the inherent violence which inevitably plagues such lawless camps.

There are many abandoned buildings and warehouses, even closed military installations, which could easily be converted to provide a temporary roof over people's heads until more permanent accommodations can be secured for them. Non-profit groups, food banks, and perhaps some churches would undoubtedly volunteer their time, help, and resources to help make any lives better.

But it all depends on whether civic leaders choose to ignore the reality of homelessness, or take the positive steps necessary to provide a just, humane solution to the problem.

WHO WILL OBJECT:

Perhaps some civic leaders and local businesses who hope and pray the problem will just go away all by itself.

<u>HUMAN RIGHTS</u>

THE PROBLEM:

Countries not following accepted Human Rights standards should not be funded with money and/or weapons.

PRACTICAL SOLUTIONS:

Imposing monetary and weapons sanctions on any Governments around the world which do not comply with basic Human Rights laws sends a powerful message. If other countries agree to fund it instead, then so be it.

Saudi Arabia and some other Middle East countries are the best examples of the problem. From a political standpoint they may be a good market for our defense industry contractors but that should not dictate true American policy as countries will exploit this arrangement in order to validate or ignore their Human Rights issues.

Many other countries in Central and South America, Eastern Europe, Asia, and much of Africa are also at fault. Giving anything to these countries outside of humanitarian aid due to natural disasters makes no sense. Subsidizing totalitarian regimes, regardless of any strategic importance claimed, only enforces their continued rule and does nothing to dissipate the harm being done to their people.

Here in America, to be completely real, we must also address our own often glossed over internal human rights issues, which are mostly in direct connection with criminal justice reform and racial discrimination.

WHO WILL OBJECT:

Foreign countries who believe their cultural laws and religious views supersede any global human rights initiatives.

IMMIGRATION & CITIZENSHIP

THE PROBLEM:

The subjects of Immigration and Citizenship have become cultural flashpoints without any practical solutions.

PRACTICAL SOLUTIONS:

There have always been many competing ideas on how to control the issue of illegal immigration into America. One embraced in conservative circles is to track down and round up any people who have entered the country illegally, throw them in jail, and deport them to their country of origin as quickly as possible. Better yet, separate children from their parents when they cross the border and toss them in cages. After all, they came in illegally.

Another idea is to give those who are already here, regardless of how and when they got in, a better path to citizenship unless they have committed a violent crime. The more Practical Solution is to embrace this direction.

America was successfully created solely through immigration and the great cultural diversity it has brought to our society. Due to political infighting and a slew of poor policies America has lost its way as a beacon for the dispossessed of the world hoping to find a safer life for their families.

This can be corrected by implementing a very Practical Solution for implementing a true and fair path to citizenship. Unlike what some racist or isolationist political pundits are quick to loudly claim, the very high majority of immigrants entering the United States, including those under the DACA arrangement, have absolutely no criminal intent in coming here. They are not murderers or rapists or criminals. Simply people hoping to find a safe haven to raise their families and be productive members of society, just like all the rest of us.

To be fair to the same American ideals which allowed people of all races to enter America and make it stronger, we must institute a more progressive approach to citizenship while completely removing from the decision making process those who preach that all who are not of their race, gender, language or religion are barred from entering our country.

To those seeking safe harbor here at our borders, what does it really portray to them about America when families and their children are separated and put into cages? It is cruel, unusual, and morally depraved punishment which must end. Those responsible should be publicly chastised and removed from any further authority over the care of human beings.

Here is a brand new Immigration and Naturalization process to follow. One that makes perfect sense. Let's call it the 2 step 2 year path to citizenship:

The Green Card lottery system should be capped at 100,000 new residents yearly, which means a million new immigrants every ten years. Green Cards should last for only one year, whereupon candidates qualify through means testing for full citizenship within one year more.

What must certainly frustrate anyone Undocumented residents who have entered the country anytime through expired visas or by any other means will be granted immunity from prosecution or deportation if they can prove to have paid taxes, can pass a background check, and have not committed any serious crimes during their stay here. All those who meet these qualifications, as well as special case refugees, will move into a Fast Track Green Card program which will go into effect immediately after they qualify. The rest of the path to full citizenship will remain the same, except with a maximum combined waiting period of only one year.

Should the issue for qualification be in relation to tax payments, non-citizens may then receive a one year probation period in order to pay taxes and then qualify under a new program, with one year to a green card and another year to full citizenship.

Any undocumented residents currently serving time in jail or prison will be subject to immediate deportation, even before their sentence ends. This will be a very good deterrent to anyone who may be contemplating the pursuit of any criminal activity within our borders. The Justice Department and Homeland Security must place an increased emphasis on who enters the country, even legally, is how long the path to citizenship really takes. The interminable wait to become a citizen is one of the reasons why the problem of undocumented non-citizens actually exists in the first place. Yes, it will entail more money and resources to make it happen, but far less than the huge amounts now being spent on failed policies.

Employers who still continue to pay undocumented workers, but not pay their taxes must be subject to increased scrutiny and fines, possible asset seizure, and even the loss of any occupational licenses.

WHO WILL OBJECT:

Racists, Isolationists, Supremacists, and some Politicians who may be supportive of either those groups, or their political need to scare the population with falsehoods..

<u>INFRASTRUCTURE</u>

THE PROBLEM:
The deterioration of America's aging infrastructure must be corrected sooner than later.

PRACTICAL SOLUTIONS:
It is amazing that in America, supposedly one of the most modern, innovative countries in the world, we lag so far behind many other developed nations in terms of infrastructure development. Our infrastructure includes roads and highways, airports, our electrical energy grid, urban development, and all the prevalent environmental concerns.

Take for example the reality of High Speed Rail. It is a definite necessity to improve our outdated, inefficient Amtrak system and reduce the prevalent non-electric transportation pollution. High Speed Rail is also a great job creator. It may be expensive to implement, but if most of Asia and Europe had the resources and initiative to do it and we have not, then why?

Clearly because of Congressional involvement, and their miserably ineffective control of Amtrak, as well as old railroad baron land politics which must be circumvented by any means possible, including eminent domain. Proponents have all the routes mapped out. It is much less environmentally disturbing than air or road travel and a good 200 MPH option. Airline lobbyists do not want this ever to happen.

Private enterprise companies can reduce the cost of doing many things and improve the technology just as they have with Outer Space, where rockets, satellites, and future space travel are taking great steps forward because the ineffective government bureaucracies are for the most part stepping aside in the face of better, more affordable realities.

Another good example is with Road Engineering like it is done in Germany with steel grids underneath the surface of autobahns to make the roads last much longer, be safer, and not be subject to expensive repairs every few years. No jobs will be lost doing this as the work to upgrade all highways across the country will actually create more jobs.

A renewable Energy Grid through development of powerful batteries, solar and wind power, will help replace an old, vulnerable, susceptible power grid definitely on its last creaky legs. Rates, pollution, and blackouts are increasing; and the system will inevitably fail across the country with tragic results financially for everyone involved.

Low Income Housing should also be considered as an infrastructure project as it will provide modern, safe, affordable residences. Nothing like the old dangerous public housing projects being torn down for replacement.

WHO WILL OBJECT:

Amtrak and its supporters, plus energy companies and their shareholders.

<u>THE INTERNET</u>

THE PROBLEM:
Affordable Internet access is not available to everyone who really needs it.

PRACTICAL SOLUTIONS:
The Internet is a curious phenomenon, and a very essential mechanism for people to connect with knowledge and each other. The pandemic in 2020 proved everyone with children needed internet access for them to still learn. But the cost to do so was unwarranted.

A few well-placed satellites in orbit could create a nationwide wi-fi system for everyone, especially students who are socially or rurally distanced from onsite learning, as well as Seniors on a fixed income. If the satellites are not up there already then they could be very soon should private enterprises get the Federal Government clearance to do so.

If internet connection could be processed digitally, low income people would not have to pay monthly internet charges they cannot afford, and their content could even be accessed over their television set on a digital antenna if they can't afford a computer. Streaming should be available to all who need it. The Internet could also qualify as an infrastructure improvement.

WHO WILL OBJECT:
Cable companies presently profiting from the service without any real price controls.

JOB CREATION

THE PROBLEM:

More domestic job creation incentives are needed to lift the economy up.

PRACTICAL SOLUTIONS:

When people have money to spend they create the whole supply and demand framework which fuels economies. When they don't, unemployment, poverty, and homelessness prevail. Lower paying service jobs do not ever accomplish changing this framework. Higher paying manufacturing jobs are what defines the true value of any job or the products and services created by it which benefit the economy.

How do we implement more job creation? First by incorporating National Infrastructure projects for better roads, high speed rail, a much better electrical grid system, and domestic manufacturing incentives to greatly reduce trade deficits, allow massive new low income housing projects, and a fairer taxation program for all.

We must promote more American manufactured jobs by increasing tax breaks for American companies to start manufacturing domestically rather than sending jobs overseas..

WHO WILL OBJECT:

Companies who are currently exporting American jobs overseas and the politicians who support their efforts.

THE JUDICIARY

THE PROBLEM:
Lifetime appointments for Federal Judges is a definite liability for the country.

PRACTICAL SOLUTIONS:
Federal Judges, even if they are on the Supreme Court level, are merely just political appointees, and as such, should be strictly held to term limits and removal proceedings.

Nominating and politically confirming judges should be vetted by an impartial body. Politicians simply do not possess the knowledge or integrity to do either effectively. Regardless of any committee assignments they may have.

Judges on the Federal level, including the Supreme Court, should still be nominated, but then thoroughly qualified by an independent panel; and then only confirmed through a National Election as appointments are not nearly fair to anyone due to partisan party objectives. They should also be held to Term Limits.

Lifetime appointments for people who make judicial decisions and are political appointees is wrong, as far too many unqualified jurists remain in positions they simply do not deserve to be in forever, or perhaps never.

WHO WILL OBJECT:
Usual suspects like the President, Congress and Federal Judges.

LABOR & UNIONS

THE PROBLEM:

Labor Unions have been beneficial to America but their power and influence still needs to be controlled in order to save American jobs they have helped lose.

PRACTICAL SOLUTIONS:

Sorry to break the news to those who may not want to hear it, but the political influence and demands of all the manufacturing and service unions in our country have directly led to the loss of manufacturing jobs. Like it or not, argue against this assumption if you will, but this is precisely what has happened. So many previously prosperous cities dependent on manufacturing companies to fuel the local economy are now almost like ghost towns. The government should have acted sooner to restrict companies from moving operations overseas where wages are substantially lower and profits could keep their products competitive, but didn't until it was too late for many destroyed communities. Due to lobbying perhaps?

Even now, companies are hesitant to relocate back into the United States unless they can get a hot deal from a progressive thinking Right-To-Work state where union pressure can be at least minimized somewhat, and where tax incentives are the trade-off for jobs.

In the United States some companies could not move their operations overseas, like say in Las Vegas where the businesses are hotels and restaurants. There is a powerful culinary union there which could strike and possibly delay a visitor's entrance if their ever increasing wage and benefit demands are not met.

All the big hotels had theme restaurants staffed by union cooks and servers, many of whom they couldn't get rid of no matter how poorly they performed. The quality was not well received by guests and income fell far below the operator's expectations, and so they were forced to adjust in a bold yet eventually necessary series of smart moves.

First, they decided to close down underperforming themed rooms and then lease out the space to well-known celebrity chefs whose operations were not subject to union influence. The new tenants actually paid their personnel much better than the mostly untalented union crews could demand. The food and service quality improved dramatically as did the profitability, and other properties quickly noticed the trend and followed suit. Today each property still has a few unionized lower cost operations; but most of the action, interest, and profits come from the non-unionized rooms which are now truly gourmet in nature. Customers like that.

It was very necessary once upon a time for unions to provide necessary wage controls to keep workers from living in poverty conditions imposed by greedy business owners, but the system was corrupted by the money and power generated by and from union officials. Many union pension plans have been lost due to poor management of their investments, as none of those in charge of those funds had any real clue on how to analyze or protect them.

Right-To-Work State amendments have helped to stem some of the union problems, since in the 27 current Right-To-Work States unions can still operate, but workers cannot be compelled to join a union as a requirement to keep their job. This restricts actual union power in those States, which makes them more attractive to any new business expansion. Most companies offer wages and benefits above the usual union demands, but without the monthly union dues (2.5 times the members hourly rate), or any unwanted union interference into the company's daily operations.

So why aren't all American States Right-To-Work through statutes? Makes you wonder, doesn't it? The simple answer is it is all about money. Unions have great political power in some States and Congress as they can financially support the election campaigns of those who support their interests. Unions also support politicians who would like to limit the control Right-To-Work States may have. Campaign finance reform can legitimately correct this problem.

There are still large powerful unions in the United States that are here to stay and will continue to factor into how industries are allowed to operate. Over 3.5 million educators belong to one of the two Teachers unions. 3.35 million belong to the Service Employees Unions which serves Healthcare workers and public service employees. Other big unions are the Teamsters, Food & Commercial, the United Auto Workers, the International Brotherhood of Electricians, Steelworkers, Construction Laborers, Police and Correctional Officers.

It is not really a matter of whether or not these unions are needed, as they do offer labor protection, decent wages, and solid benefits for their members. The real defining issue is how these unions have actually affected the loss of manufacturing jobs in the United States, and how non Right-To-Work States will ever be able to compete with Right-To-Work States when the Federal Government eventually takes steps to force American companies to financially reconsider their lucrative offshore ventures.

WHO WILL OBJECT:

Union leaders, political puppets, and some union members.

LAND MANAGEMENT

THE PROBLEM:
The Federal Government controls far too much land.

PRACTICAL SOLUTIONS:
The Bureau of Land Management (BLM) controls almost 20% of the land mass in America, over 150 million acres. Land is mostly leased out for livestock grazing to bring in over $6 billion in annual revenue, and is politically controlled by those who benefit from it.

Except for National Parks or Military areas the Federal Government should not control any other land. It should be turned over to the States, with some environmental restrictions. States should be able to staff and administer National Parks in their area to eliminate the Federal bureaucracy, including a myriad of field offices around the country. It would also be a welcome financial boon to the States involved. Few jobs would be lost in transition as States would be inclined to hire Park Service people already working there.

Many National Parks are much larger than needed and acreage could be significantly reduced without destroying the integrity of any park features. States could then determine what best to do with excess land, subject to laws.

Another important issue involving land management is the very controversial usage of fracking to chemically extract natural gas. Landowners are unwillingly forced to accept fracking on their land but most fail to support the process even though they have been given financial incentives to do so. This natural gas extraction method should only be limited to unoccupied State or Federal lands where people are not to be affected by any of the adverse effects the chemical procedure causes.

People may own the land where their homes and farms are but the Government claims they don't own what is below ground and can somehow justify leasing out that land to corporations who pump chemicals into the ground. Natural gas production may well be important to our energy reliance, and also lucrative for the companies doing the fracking.

Environmental concerns are currently being dismissed as they may endanger profiteering. Homeowners affected by fracking are being exposed to undrinkable well water, bad even poisonous air, and a myriad of resulting health problems. The industry discounts these claims as they have seemingly paid to have the political protection to do whatever they so desire. Future Fracking leases should be approved by the EPA, current leases should be thoroughly reviewed by the EPA as well, and dissolved if conditions warrant doing so.

WHO WILL OBJECT:
The BLM, the National Park Service, the Interior Department, politicians with a vested interest, and all those fracking companies.

LGBTQ RIGHTS

THE PROBLEM:

Discrimination against LGBTQ people must end.

PRACTICAL SOLUTIONS:

The LGBTQ Equality Act should be a priority for all lawmakers in Congress as it will ensure the enforcement of hates crimes and discrimination penalties. This should be a zero tolerance policy, by law. Whether someone else has a different gender or sexual identity should not be the concern of anyone else. It has nothing to do with anyone's religious beliefs or any prevailing sense of morality.

This is not about being transphobic or anything else, as any of that is inherently discrimination. Even if some of us are not personally a part of any of these persuasions, it must be recognized they are just people wanting to be free and happy, certainly not in any way a threat to anyone else.

If someone doesn't like these people or what they stand for, such is their prerogative to do so. But to act towards them or in any negative way personally or professionally is not. They are not after the affections or attention of their detractors in any way. They may want little to do with others or what they think unless they can be accepted for who and what they really are. Just people like all the rest of us.

They are someone's sons or daughters or brothers and sisters, cousins, friends, or maybe even mothers and fathers. So just stay silent, walk away if what you see or hear bothers you, and most importantly please do both the straight world and the pride world a big favor by minding your own damn business. They whom some of you are somehow afraid of, disgusted by, or intimidated by, really won't mind if you do just that. In fact, they will probably rejoice in it. Maybe even feel some Pride.

What anyone does with their body or with someone else, as long as they adhere to sensible common law, is of their own concern and never in any way anyone else's. Those identifying as LGBTQ are mostly confident, happy, and proud people in their lifestyle, who they have chosen to be, and whom they have chosen to love. Anyone feeling somehow morally superior to others should probably just connect their hatred to its true source, which is definitely just a nasty pile of fecal ignorance.

One issue needing further resolution has to do with transgender individuals and whether gender identity or actual birth gender will be the determining factor regarding the issues of restroom use and fair athletic competition. Testosterone laced boys competing against real girls in competition is patently unfair.

WHO WILL OBJECT:
You know who you are.

THE LINE ITEM VETO

THE PROBLEM:

America can't afford wasting money it doesn't have on pork barrel projects.

PRACTICAL SOLUTIONS:

The Line Item Veto is a measure which is long overdue but hasn't been implemented since Congress does not want to give this power to any President. But this is a must to balance the budget and reduce the Federal deficit by eliminating partisan pork barrel projects lawmakers slip into huge Omnibus bills often as a compromise to get their support.

Usually these totally wasteful additions are sponsored by lawmakers trying to benefit the State they represent. There is little value in these pork, which never benefits America as a whole.

If granted to the Executive branch it should not be overridden except by a 60% SuperMajority of both houses of Congress. Once lawmakers realize the time and effort they spend dreaming up untenable projects will just be in vain, it might prompt them to show more job integrity and develop more beneficial legislation on a timely basis not currently seen.

WHO WILL OBJECT:

Various lawmakers of political parties who believe it is their inherent right to waste money on pet projects.

<u>LOBBYISTS</u>

THE PROBLEM:

Lobbyist money being regularly sent to legislators clearly amounts to legalized bribery.

PRACTICAL SOLUTIONS:

Even though there are Constitutional precepts and Supreme Court decisions allowing for lobbyists to legally do just that, it is still wrong. In civil courts and even Federal proceedings this would amount to a crime subject to prosecution. But not so in Congress.

The Founding Fathers could never foresee how big a business and influence the lobbying industry would become. As for SCOTUS, their decisions, including those regarding lobbyists, are all too often merely partisan based decisions.

The only way to firmly control the undue influence of lobbyists and eliminate the money they can route through Political Action Committees into re-election campaigns is to severely limit what they can actually do.

Money is not really free speech, unless as we have explained before that it somehow literally flows out of someone's mouth when they speak. Figuratively that is what happens according to lawmakers and jurists, but in truth it is not a valid or literal scenario in any way.

Lobbyists simply deal in bribery and/or extortion. If PAC tributes are strictly reduced through the Federal Election Commission, or better yet eliminated by the Public Funding of Elections, this will help shelve the influence lobbyist money has over lawmakers, and affirmatively what laws and special interests they can support with their cash.

Lobbyists are part of a very large influence industry, but they are not the real true constituents of any elected Congressional members. Yet they are allowed to act as if they are, without impunity. Wrong, dead wrong.

WHO WILL OBJECT:

Lobbyists and the politicians who profit from them.

MILITARY AFFAIRS

THE PROBLEM:
We spend more on our military than any other country, and also waste more funds than any other country.

PRACTICAL SOLUTIONS:
America is lauded to have the most powerful military in the world, which is a good thing. For this honor we spend far more than any other country in the world. Over 12% of America's budget is spent on Defense, which consumes 55% of the nation's entire Discretionary Spending fund.

Yet warfare and defense hawks cry out that our military capabilities are eroding and we must throw more money at the problem to fix it. This is not the case and nothing could actually be further from the truth. There is more than enough funds already allocated to satisfy America's Defense goals. Targeting that 12% down to 10% or less, and lowering that 55% to below 50% will actually strengthen the Military.

The real problem is how all the money is actually being spent. Far too much financial waste is generated in the military bureaucracy and its defense industry partners which could be controlled better, and then utilized for future development.

The truly sad and dysfunctional Military procurement process, which hasn't seemed to ever be overseen by any competent management programs, wastes millions, perhaps billions of budget dollars annually. As a prime example, contracts with weapons manufacturers always seem to include provisions for unseen cost overruns, which magically always seem to occur, greatly inflating the final cost of purchases on a regular basis. This is no way to run a successful business, but that is actually how the Defense Department operations should be run, like the big business it actually is.

For some incomprehensible reasons Congressional lawmakers seem to think they have more expertise in what the military needs than what military professionals do. That doesn't make sense since no one in Congress is actually a military expert, despite the overseeing committee they may have been assigned to. Even if they served in the military it does not make them expert on anything of significance.

Congress members still inexplicably control the reins to legislate the military into purchasing equipment manufactured in their home State; which may not actually be wanted or needed. The legislators could probably care less what happens to that equipment as their principal interest was in successfully wrangling a very lucrative contract for their State. Congress should not be allowed to approve any military equipment purchases, or deny any purchases desired by the Armed Forces without a 60% SuperMajority approval vote.

The Military is saddled with an abundance of higher ranking officers whose pay grades clearly outmatch current usefulness, partially due to old Cold War staffing objectives no longer necessary. At the same time, rank and file service members on the front lines of all conflicts risk their lives for a mere pittance of an officer's salary, and families are forced to live in often squalid conditions below poverty levels.

Congress consistently stands in the way of closing unneeded domestic military bases and turning over the land and upkeep expenses to States or local governments who can modify the property for better purposes. Due again to the Cold War stigma there are far too many military bases around the world which should be consolidated or closed. Do we need a multitude of military installations in places like Germany when only a few are necessary? Definitely not. The Cold War is in the past and future conflicts will be much different than expected before. Foreign bases are also very expensive to run.

Another huge waste is in the Department of Defense which employs hundreds of thousands of expensive sub-contractors when our servicemen and women could be trained to do those jobs more efficiently and economically.

What could be done with these cost savings? The first step would be to immediately raise enlisted pay grades up at least 10% with guaranteed annual Cost of Living increases. Higher deserved wages and shorter deployment rotations make for happier service people and their families, thus reducing the high divorce and suicide rates prevalent in our Armed Forces which are not being advertised publicly.

There is the very pertinent question of whether a man wearing a football helmet or a baseball glove, dribbling a basketball or swinging a hockey stick, should be making so much more than a soldier wearing a helmet and defending our country. The answer is very clear.

The Navy will continue to focus on building smaller carriers to carry attack helicopters and Vertical Takeoff and Landing planes; instead of producing larger, more expensive, and more targetable super aircraft carriers, which we already have more than enough of. Using smaller, less expensive and more maneuverable ships will actually enhance our sea presence anywhere around the world, and they can also be used to transport USMC Rapid Deployment forces. The Navy should continue developing an armada of drone submarines and warships. Explosive long range rail guns will also be part of any future modifications, even on drones.

Marines will continue to remain the principal American fighting force in future conflicts. Their active duty and reserve personnel numbers should be increased, as should wages, weapons capability, and use of drone attack planes to provide ground support. Rapid Deployment forces must remain combat ready and deployable anywhere in the world on short notice.

The Army will continue to be mainly responsible for the heavy duty tank, artillery, and ground forces needed. Do not be surprised to see more unmanned weaponry, including lethal drone tanks joining the Army arsenal.

The Air Force will continue to upgrade its fleet with next Generation attack planes and also a greater emphasis on UAV drone warfare. Our game playing children of today could well be the great drone pilots of tomorrow, and they will be ready and willing if called.

What will the military actually do around the world? As stated in Foreign Affairs, the smartest thing to do is for America to stay out of other countries' conflicts unless they directly threaten our country or an ally. We are not the world's sheriff and cannot afford to be. If drawn into a fight then we must be prepared to react quickly, and with the overwhelming force we have paid dearly to acquire.

WHO WILL OBJECT:

Defense contractors, the DOD, older military officers, and politicians who think they know better. Enlisted personnel and their families will likely not object very much at all.

<u>MINIMUM WAGES</u>

THE PROBLEM:

The current Federal Minimum Wage invites poverty.

PRACTICAL SOLUTIONS:

The current $7.25 Federal minimum wage heading into 2021 really only serves to keep people in poverty, where they may need to seek social services and/or Food stamps to help them survive. Our country must move ahead and institute a gradual $15.00 minimum wage for all Federal jobs, or with companies doing business with the Federal Government. A Cost of Living annual adjustment should then be a fair and mandatory part of the system. If adjusted to today's prices through COLA the minimum would be about $25.00 an hour.

Some States, mostly in the Deep South, do not even have any minimum wage number. They should be advised that if they don't raise the State minimum to at least the Federal level they will surely lose essential service workers to other more amenable States. The effect this will have is some businesses may no longer qualify for Federal contracts because they do not provide a true living wage for their employees. This will wind up costing conservative States in the western Rocky Mountains, parts of the Midwest, and the Deep South a pretty penny;

but it is necessary to combat poverty caused by greed, and the public assistance it creates.

Going from $7.25 to $10.00 per hour initially is a reasonable first step. Then going up $1.25 each year until $15.00 an hour is reached will be easier for employers and the economy to handle. Tying further increases into the Cost of Living index solidifies the plan so the discussion going forward becomes moot.

Employers and businesses may continue to spout the fallacy that higher wages result in job losses, and will create higher prices. So what if a hamburger or chicken sandwich goes up a quarter or two? This is known as inflation and it has always been with us, and it always will be. Sometimes businesses do it to raise profits, and sometimes to keep their bottom line more profitable. If the very convenient falsehood about wages destroying jobs was actually true, then more of us would be living in abject poverty, which the very wealthy might welcome, or perhaps not even care about at all.

Another aspect of Minimum Wage restructuring would be to abolish the current Wage Decrease Provision for tipped employees in restaurants and hotels. That egregious $2.15 an hour plus tips system has been rife with abuses from greedy employers for many years and needs to be destroyed.

WHO WILL OBJECT:
Business owners, some restaurants, but very few if any employees will object.

NATIONAL REFERENDUMS

THE PROBLEM:
With Congress unwilling to correct their self-inflicted abuses, the need for National Referendums becomes clear.

PRACTICAL SOLUTIONS:
In most elections, it is usually what happens at the ballot box which shows what Americans really want. But national elections in America are normally just limited to candidates, and not to any of the major issues of importance.

In our political system the process of initiatives and referendums does allow the citizens of a good many States to actually place new legislation on a popular ballot, or rescind recently passed legislation. Surprisingly enough there is no actual provision for holding referendums at the Federal level because the Constitution does not explicitly provide for it. Why? A salient guess is our Founding Fathers either did not understand the principle, or thought it wouldn't be needed.

Actually, our failure to introduce Direct Democracy for national issues in 2021 after a 245 year history of not doing so is very strange to say the least. But now it is definitely needed.

Currently over 20 States across our country, plus many local and city governments who provide for the adoption of citizen initiatives and referendums. These have proven popular with the citizenry as a whole as it gives them a real say in the issues which directly affect their lives. The concept of allowing this approval system is also referred to as Direct Democracy, and in truth expanding this onto a national scale is a very natural and necessary step which will actually make our Constitutional structure even more Democratic.

States have found that their citizens have responded to unfamiliar or unfair political legislation with some anger as they feel clearly distanced from the decision making process. It has been said there needs to be a very vital bridge between those who are the rulers and those they rule. Direct Democracy is the true road to that bridge. It is a way for citizens to address their concerns over major issues in a constructive manner which hopefully makes the Government more responsible.

A vast majority of countries in every region of the world allow for National Referendums, so it is definitely not a new concept. Pollsters also report that more than two-thirds of Americans greatly support the idea of Direct Democracy as they can see how Congress is failing the country.

The process to allow for National Referendums may not be fast or easy. The quickest way of course, would be for Congress to approve a Constitutional Amendment to allow this, which many lawmakers may oppose as it might seemingly limit their legislative powers, which it definitely is intended to do. So don't hold your breath. An Executive Branch decree from a truly progressive President could move this process along, if such a brave President ever comes to power. But some necessary baby steps towards the goal are more than likely, and those take time and perseverance. Nonetheless, the process is doable and therefore those steps must be taken for the benefit of everyone in our country. It would not necessarily include amending the Constitution in order to do so.

Scholars have mapped out several key steps to bring this all about. The first step would be to introduce a series of non-binding Referendums to Federal elections every two year cycle. Meaning, we get to see a consensus on issues that are not actually binding by law, but still important to American citizens as a whole. This could be on anything from legislature to social issues or foreign affairs. It is testing the waters so to speak, to find out the true will of the people.

The next step would be to grant citizens the absolute right to gather signatures to add more non-binding issues, or Referenda onto National ballots. Many countries in Europe already do this, with enthusiastic support from their citizenry.

If Congress truly does serve the will of the general population and not just special interest groups, their members should use the referendum results to introduce supporting legislation to address any number of important topics. For candidates in elections, those who do support the results of those referenda will certainly gain support at the ballot box

When, not if, referendums prove to be popular, then it will be time for America to follow much of the approach California has already taken. This State has one of the largest economies in the world and is very progressive politically. Their Direct Democracy allows for binding Referendums on initiatives to change laws and adopt amendments that are adopted from the direct votes of their electorate.

There are those who will argue there are hidden risks in adopting a Direct Democracy tool. Some may say that instituting a National Referendum policy will be divisive, as if Congress and the rest of the country aren't already sailing in those very separate boats in opposite directions. It has been documented much to the contrary, as this provides for adoption of the direct will of the people who don't have to be beholden to party politics in order to express what they feel is needed.

It has also been observed that even in some very Catholic countries like Italy and Ireland, the Referendum system has managed issues such as legalized abortion better than we ever have, because the results were determined by the will and power of the citizens involved themselves. Not by politicians.

Also not true is the idea that Direct Democracy would promote extremism. Actually the opposite is true, since voting is by majority rule and research shows voters are much less extreme in their personal views than what political propaganda may implore them to be.

The bottom line to this extremely credible movement is to keep America a Democracy, and common sense provides that the best way to do so is to simply practice Democracy more. Referendums and Direct Democracy give more of us who are not involved in the sometimes corrupt and usually divisive political system now in place, a well deserved say in all the important matters which so greatly affect our lives.

WHO WILL OBJECT:

Politicians, Lobbyists, Special Interest Groups.

<u>NATIVE AMERICAN AFFAIRS</u>

THE PROBLEM:

How our Federal Government has continually been treating Native Americans is a National shame.

PRACTICAL SOLUTIONS:

The original indigenous Americans have long been kept in a subservient role by the intrepid settlers who came to this country, and the Government which evolved to virtually enslave them. Today, ever so sadly, if a Native American Indian tribe is not empowered to run a gambling casino, the surrounding community is usually left in abject poverty.

The American Indian tribal culture is a great and diverse one; and many towns, cities, rivers, States, and other areas in America remain named based upon what the Native Americans called those places. In fact, a lot of sports teams in both high school, college, and professional sports proudly use references to valiant Indian warriors in their nicknames.

Yet proud Native American peoples are still treated like second class citizens in America, a shameful designation reflecting very badly upon both our Federal Government and Congressional lawmakers. We as a Nation must persevere to give back to Native Americans what we have taken from them, both in land and most importantly of all, their dignity.

The Bureau of Indian Affairs is a very small part of the Federal Interior Department, and while having lofty goals to help improve the lives and living conditions of the over 500 recognized American Indian tribes, persistent underfunding of the Bureau's budget relegates those lofty goals down into just wishful thinking. The BIA should be a separate Federal Department in order to truly be beneficial to those it serves.

A number of relevant actions can and should be taken to correct the country's disservice to Native Americans. The Department of Education can help improve Indian K-12 schools and colleges, or fund the necessary resources to help students assimilate into other non-Indian schools off reservation land. Free State college tuition will go a long way toward showing young Native Americans clear hope, and the realization they are recognized as a vital part of American society, and not as second class citizens.

Small business incentives should be created to lure manufacturing businesses to lease Indian land and employ trainable people who now may only be able to live in a community of welfare poverty. In terms of mental health and drug and alcohol treatment programs, more help should be forthcoming. Medicare and Medicaid coverage should be available to all, with modern on-site clinics or access to them.

So far only a handful of Native Americans have ever tried to run for public office or even been employed by the Federal Government. Since diversity has always been and will always be important to America, more emphasis should be shown to encourage Native Americans to enter civil or political service. This will help give Native Americans a much stronger voice in our country.

These are the real true Americans and we should treat them with honor as such. Until this very unsavory situation is rectified, then the old Indian adage of "White Man Speak With Forked Tongue" will continue to ring true.

WHO WILL OBJECT:
The same political forces which have always been the true cause behind the problem.

POLICE REFORM

THE PROBLEM:

Unwarranted use of force and the killing of unarmed citizens has given the public a negative opinion of all police.

PRACTICAL SOLUTIONS:

Make no mistake about it, the vast majority of police officers serving the public really are the good guys. Are there a few bad apples among them whose actions give the rest of the officers and their public identity a disrespectful image to some citizens? Yes indeed, and these instances are continuing to be exposed at an ever alarming rate.

Some officers involved in these incidents may have violent tendencies or inherent racial biases to provoke them in a violent way. Often, the public doesn't know what to expect if confronted by police, especially depending on their skin color.

Congress must endeavor to create a Federal Police Commission, perhaps through the Department of Justice to investigate all questionable killings, eliminate the intolerable defenses provided by powerful police unions to protect their members, and definitely change the departmental culture everywhere. Saying that an officer somehow felt threatened by someone not brandishing a gun, or that they had to shoot and kill a fleeing suspect, is never an acceptable excuse. It should however, be a crime.

All law enforcement officers must be required to wear body cameras or face expulsion. This alone will help control any divisive prejudices these officers may entertain. It is vital for all police departments and associations to regain the public trust. This can only be done by example, and by making sure all officers rigidly follow careful procedures to eliminate most of these incidents from ever happening again.

Officers who do not follow stricter protocol should be fired and then face criminal charges just like anyone else in America who commits a crime. Some police departments are reporting an exodus of officers who object to the public portrayal of their methods and the resulting loss of morale it brings to their department. Be careful to not let the door kick their rear ends too hard on the way out the door.

WHO WILL OBJECT:
Police Departments, Police Unions, and some Officers.

POLITICAL PARTIES

THE PROBLEM:

Having a very slight majority in any political theatre should not be considered a consensus in any way.

PRACTICAL SOLUTIONS:

In most major national elections our country always votes almost half Democrat and half Republican, with not enough other party candidates to ever make a real difference. It never truly allows for good election choices.

In 2016 did you vote for Clinton or Trump, neither of whom were really palatable to everyone? Clinton wins the popular vote but Trump gets the Electoral vote. Is everyone really happy with however the result could have turned out to be, or is this in any way a mandate for anyone to govern as they please? Most Americans will say it is not, regardless of who was relegated to the throne. The choices in many elections are not good either way.

The real solution is the creation of a strong third party alternative. As the Republican and Democrat parties stand opposed today, one party casts the other as dangerous leftist socialists, snowflakes, perhaps even communists. The other side counters their opponents are violent right wing extremists, racists, and insurrectionists. If we actually divide the electorate into true left wing liberals and true right wing conservatives, we will probably find no more than maybe 15% are true socialist liberals or true right wing extremists.

The rest of the electorate seems to vote along their party line so as to not be identified with the evil left and right extremists they have been programmed to fear. But studies show most voters favor a centrist approach to issues. The bottom line is most of us should just be designated as Independents not subject to any misleading propaganda or pressure by either major party. To alleviate this situation a viable Third or Independent party must be supported to include moderates and progressives who do not align their beliefs with either the extreme left or right. They meet in the center where the resolution of issues is easier to come by.

A Progressive Party, where educated and moderate minded citizens can feel safe to support what will probably be a majority decision in most cases would be welcome. This will help do away with the divisive Republican and Democrat partisan gridlock failures for America, despite all the Constitutional precepts they have afforded themselves.

Realistically not one remaining political group may be able to garner 50% of the vote in a Federal election, as is the way of most of the free world, but it would appear the new middle moderate party will likely receive the majority of votes, thus leading the country away from any unwanted extremism either on the left or the right. As proven in countries throughout the world, a coalition government approach actually facilitates bi-partisanship in order to get anything meaningful done. If lawmakers don't get enough accomplished while in office, they are simply voted out.

WHO WILL OBJECT:

Political parties and extremist elements.

<u>POVERTY</u>

THE PROBLEM:

As supposedly the wealthiest and most advanced country on the Planet Earth the level of poverty in America is unacceptable, if not truly unfathomable.

PRACTICAL SOLUTIONS:

In a true capitalist system the rich always get richer and the poor always get poorer, but in a democratic society those imbalances have to be subsidized until they can be corrected. Jobs and decent wages will help do that.

To be honest, the current Federal Poverty Levels are at least 20% below where they should be as the parameters they base their levels on are not inclusive of all the existing circumstances of the unprecedented rises in both housing and food costs. Once improved, a true Federal Poverty Level will help all of those financially dispossessed by poverty, especially the homeless or those on welfare.

In order to solve any of the distressing problems people in poverty face, the services and solutions needed which can help them must include both determination and heart. Those in power who do not believe in utilizing every available humanitarian resource to put an end to poverty and homelessness should subsequently be voted out of office.

There but for the grace of God is where any of us could be. Many may have lived through poverty or sleeping in cars while jobless. Perhaps some survived and eventually prospered through the help of others, or maybe just faith in themselves or a higher power. Not everyone has the strength or hope or willpower to make it out of the darkness. But there are those in society who can light the way ahead for them. Leaders and lawmakers need to act from their heart, and not worry about the cost to elicit meaningful change.

One of the most truly distressing aspects of poverty is that here in America over 20 million children still live in poverty. This is disgraceful on many levels, truly the most disgusting of which is that politicians and lawmakers think the cost of rectifying the problem outweighs the benefit. This thinking may be construed as racially motivated.

Again we must be reminded that most of these elected officials don't really give a damn on many issues unless it graces their re-election coffers. But here are some of the true costs of keeping children in poverty as they grow up: hopelessness, crime, drug use, violence, incarceration, and lives lost. The benefit does clearly outweigh the cost.

The actual cost to society by not subsidizing an end to poverty, is the critical effect that keeping people in poverty has on substantially lowering the long term economic impact these citizens can have on both themselves and the country. The true cost of stabilizing or eradicating poverty clearly outweighs any political arguments regarding the financing necessary to resolve the problem.

WHO WILL OBJECT:

Those in society who really don't care about anyone else other than themselves.

PRESIDENTIAL POWERS

THE PROBLEM:

Does an American President have too much power or not nearly enough?

PRACTICAL SOLUTIONS:

This is a tough call since there is a need to give some more powers to the President for the good of the country, but also the need to take away a few that can and have been abused to the detriment of the country.

In the President's favor a Line Item Veto of wasteful Congressional spending bills has been a must for a very long time, and should only be able to be overturned by a 60% SuperMajority vote. In addition, no Presidential Executive orders should be implemented or overturned except by a SuperMajority 60% vote.

We must strive to greatly limit the scope of Presidential pardons to not include political allies, any relatives of the president, convicted murderers, treasonists, or felons; plus any possible preemptive pardons.

The President should also not be able to use their own Justice Department to defend the Executive Branch against any criminal prosecutions against them while in office. Sorry, but the DOJ is not intended to be the personal defense team of the Executive Branch.

Most presidents, even with their trusted advisers, are definitely not military experts, or unfortunately sometimes not even experienced Government leaders. Winning what is often just a political popularity contest should not give any incoming President free reign to do whatever they want, especially as it directly affects Constitutional law. True Democracy relying on the court system prevents autocrats rather than encouraging any degree of dictatorship.

The President's role as the Commander in Chief over the Military must be closely monitored by the Joint Chiefs of Staff, who should also be able to directly appeal Congress for help in resolving any differences with the President regarding the use of any military force against foreign entities. Presidents are not military experts, regardless of what they claim.

As to be expected, Presidents would probably not be agreeable to a reduction of their broad powers, and since Congress would likely not support a Presidential Line Item Veto to remove pork barrel projects from important spending bills; then only through Direct Democracy initiatives can these very needed and essential refinements ever be achieved.

WHO WILL OBJECT:
Both the Presidency and Congress, but for much different reasons.

PRIVATIZATION

THE PROBLEM:
The Federal Government has proven to be a failure in most business ventures it controls.

PRACTICAL SOLUTIONS:
As most of America has already experienced, private enterprise can get things done much quicker, cheaper, and more efficiently than any Federal Government controlled enterprises possibly could.

Take for example the United States Postal Service which Congress operates and has to annually subsidize as a loss since Congress doesn't really seem to ever know what they are doing. In the era of internet advertising, direct deposits, and online messaging, much of society has little real need for regular mail delivery.

First class mail is the most profitable service to the USPS but its usage has dropped dramatically due to phone texting, e-mails, direct deposits, and social media. In both urban and rural areas a Monday-Wednesday-Friday delivery schedule would be totally acceptable to most, which would help reduce the USPS payroll dramatically.

The current USPS loses a lot of money annually since their revenue is far too low in accordance with the services they provide and the overhead this entails. Bulk and commercial mail has increased, which may indicate the rates for those services are far too low. Want less junk mail? Just make it more expensive to send. Package delivery continues to rise in volume, although it is not one of the most profitable areas of mail service, and other delivery companies do it far better. Getting Congress out of the control of mail service can only help but improve it. It might be more expensive utilizing something like FedEx or UPS, but the service would be better because professionals would be running it, and not politicians.

How about Amtrak, a very expensive loss leader for many years, due solely to Congressional mismanagement as none of those who are serving in Congress are really experts in anything, especially rail transportation; again despite whatever important Committees they may belong to. Some Amtrak proponents want to keep throwing more money at the problem. Maybe they'll get a station named after themselves in the process. The problem is not necessarily all the old trains, dilapidated tracks, subsidized fares, Congress, or the whole Amtrak administration. It is all of it lumped together into what is a badly inefficient business platform.

Private enterprises developing High Speed Rail modernization is the real future. Most of Europe and Asia have already found a way to update their infrastructure through high speed rail. The land is already there but railroad companies just don't want to give it up except perhaps by . eminent domain. Amtrak is definitely not the future.

Then there is the whole magnificent realm of Outer Space where private enterprises are now providing lower cost access to space travel and have quickly accomplished what the bureaucracy enveloping NASA could not ever do. Lock up creative minds in a mind-boggling bureaucracy and see why there is never enough time or money to realize the necessary advancements definitely out there waiting.

Our archaic and penultimately dangerous fossil fuel powered main electrical grid system run by so-called Public Utility companies seems to create far more environmental messes and power failures than warranted or expected. The rising instances of both rolling and total power blackouts is directly attributable to these companies' reluctance to explore and develop new energy technologies; which are completely renewable, sustainable, and possess very little if any negative environmental impact.

These are some of the main institutions in America needing to be privatized. Many other privatization options will inevitably follow, precisely as they should.

WHO WILL OBJECT:
Supporters of Amtrak, NASA, the USPS, and Public Utility Commissions.

RACIAL TENSIONS

THE PROBLEM:

Racial tensions in America are one of the worst and most divisive issues this country faces.

PRACTICAL SOLUTIONS:

In 2021 the racial demographics in America are approximately 60% White, 17% Hispanic/Latino, 13% African American, 7% Asian, and 3% other races.

Although more than over 150 years have passed since slavery legally ended, many Americans still have some very violent racist tendencies. Most are White, but some are Black, Hispanic, Asian, or Middle Eastern. The haters all make the mistake of just despising other races and skin colors, while the true color of anyone actually exists only in their heart. If you possess a black and evil heart, even though your skin may be white, then you may choose to hate anyone who is not the same color or ethnicity not only as your skin, but your heart as well.

In America to combat these ever simmering problems which sometimes boil over into inexplicable violence, we must again endeavor to strengthen and enforce all hate crime penalties. There must be an expansion of constructive community policing. There must be a prioritization of fair racial education in all schools from K-12 through community colleges and universities. Hate speech invoking violence against others should never be evaluated or accepted as "Free Speech". But it should definitely be a crime.

When the COVID-19 pandemic hit, allegations it initiated in China spurred many racist, hateful or uneducated Americans to vilify and even attack anyone who looked like an Asian as if the whole race was responsible. Hispanic immigrants fleeing to our borders for safety are treated like criminals, their children taken from them, and some in our society actually approve of this. African American people demonstrate when one of their fathers, sons or daughters are killed by white police officers while being unarmed.

Yet some in the citizenry think their protests should be silenced. What if black peace officers, of which there are many, were killing unarmed white men? Do you think this would somehow change the narrative?

In America we had President Obama for eight very peaceful years. The country ran quite smoothly under his administration, recovered from a tough recession, and he successfully kept us out of starting any more wars than others across the political aisle may have wanted. So why did Conservatives and their extremist right wing dogs and the brazen media outlets which support them try to vilify this President? It wasn't really because of his policies, but it was very definitely all about the color of his skin. Which they who are accused will emphatically deny of course, as they do with most anything which is actually truthful.

There are a lot of racist, white supremacist ideology leaning people in this country who most of us do not want as a neighbor, much less a citizen of where we live. These are not true honest Americans in any way, shape, or form. While some of us may be afraid of them, instead we must be emboldened to prevent the spread of their ideas or actions.

Racists of any color or religion are usually not really smart people since education has probably not been a main priority in life. But they are still very angry and dangerous people rooted in hateful ways. If any of them are ever exposed as a threat to anyone who doesn't align with their views then they should be treated as criminals by the proper authorities. They must definitely be vetted out of our Military, Law Enforcement, Public Service, and Correctional Officer communities; because therein may lie a lot of the problems.

Zero tolerance is the only way to fight against those who seek to use their hatred to divide a nation historically built upon the strength of its vast diversity.

WHO WILL OBJECT:
I think we have already covered that.

THE BUSINESS OF RELIGION

THE PROBLEM:

The panhandling, tax-avoiding business of religion nullifies any benefits people of faith may derive from their teachings.

PRACTICAL SOLUTIONS:

In advance we pray for your pious forgiveness, but these rich televangelists and their mega-churches have to be put into proper perspective. They don't really speak to God, they just want you to believe they do, and then they expect their faithful to pay up accordingly for the grand illusion.

Here we come to address one of the Holy Grails of American society, the true separation of Church and State. Religion in its true sense can be a blessing to all, no matter what religion anyone worships. Some avid churchgoers love to dress up each Sunday, go to church, socialize with friends, and sing praises to whatever lord they believe in as it makes them feel very good. It is all that really matters.

But let's get real and realize that giving money to any religion with their tithe hand out is never going to be a cure-all for anything. People will still die, people will still be poor, and the morals of people around the world will not likely change. Including some of those you send money too.

Religious differences have caused far more wars and brutal deaths than any other single entity in the history of this world. Whether you are Protestant, Christian, Catholic, Muslim, Hindu, Buddhist, Orthodox, or others; none of them will ever admit to that guilt, but history does not lie. From time immemorial in religious circles there has always been this mantra that if you do not believe in what I believe in, then you must be evil and destroyed. Beliefs like that still continue to raise those ugly and bloody heads even today.

Do any of you really think this is what any God of any religious persuasion has ever preached? No, humans have been the only ones who created these twisted beliefs in order to promote their own agendas for power, wealth, and conquest. No true Gods would have ever commanded this.

Today, at least in America, Churches pay virtually no taxes and some greedy evangelists have become millionaires by preying on the spiritually weak at heart. Churches should be taxed, at the very least on their property, and treated exactly like any other non-profit entity. Declaring yourself a religion is a relatively easy thing to do, but it does not make anyone or their organization, no matter how powerful, worthy of special considerations or exalted in any way. If someone preaches to you that they actually speak to God, then you'll probably buy some of their snake oil in the gift shop on your way out the door. Like politicians they want you to faithfully believe in everything they say, and show your faith by sending them money, whether you can really afford to or not. Just have faith. We talk to God.

As a truly sad example, the Catholic Church pretends to be so utterly pious, supremely high and mighty above all other religions, yet it has continually been exposed in far too many pedophile sex scandals; most of which they have tried to suppress through their political power and money influence. Yet they still get a tax break. Who are they paying off?

Many evangelical churches have also been known to carefully embrace white supremacist ideology and practice racial discrimination. For this should they receive any special considerations? Doubtful. Make that no.

Religious interpretations from various groups have also always been very convenient means to discriminate against State, Federal, and Constitutional laws on the basis of their "faith and beliefs". But in reality these arguments are really only sanctimonious nonsense, and the thinly veiled ability for them to have the freedom to discriminate against anyone else whom they do not like by ethnicity or color, or those who do not willfully contribute to their church.

No one should ever really care what anyone else worships, to whom or why. Bigotry has not been something espoused by any religion's wise loving lord and savior. In the end we must all still abide by law, except some religious institutions who seem to believe they are above those laws.

Spirituality and the belief in a Golden Rule towards life and how you treat others as you would like to be treated, should be enough of a blessing for anyone to follow on a positive path. As a plus, no 10% income tithe will ever be expected from doing the right thing for yourself and others.

The highly discriminatory and corrupt business of religion is really nothing more than a sad cruel financial hoax that neither Jesus, Mohammed, Buddha, Krishna, or any other revered religious deities would in any of their beliefs and teachings have ever condoned. Sometimes, it is simply the messengers who cannot be trusted.

WHO WILL OBJECT:
Churches, televangelists, cults, religious grifters, and religious zealots.

<u>SECESSION & SEDITION</u>

THE PROBLEM:

Following the disputed 2020 election disgruntled States posed the threat of Secession, and some lawmakers took political stances which may charge them with Sedition.

PRACTICAL SOLUTIONS:

It is nearly incomprehensible to fathom that some 139 members of the GOP House decided to back President #45's worthless election fraud claims in 2020. Why? Because the 14th Amendment to the Constitution and the oath members of Congress took upon entering this chamber clearly forbids this as an act of Sedition, which is so very close to actual treason. If prosecuted this could potentially unseat all of these Congressmen and remove them from Congress. It could happen, maybe it really should happen. Was it a smart or really dumb move for them? Duh?

Many supporters of the election loser will still not accept the fact their candidate lost, despite the multitude of court decisions affirming this. Some States have even threatened to try and secede from the Union in typical old Confederate fashion. It would probably take a 60% majority vote in any State to legally start this process. Letting disgruntled States leave the country would be more a burden to them than the remaining United States. Why?

Because Blue States send far more tax dollars to the Treasury than they receive back, while Red States consistently receive back far more than they ever contribute.

Based upon the 2020 election results here are the Red States which could empower secession with over a 60% voter approval: Idaho, Wyoming, Alabama, Arkansas, Oklahoma, South Dakota, Kentucky, Tennessee, North Dakota, West Virginia. Others at 55-60%: Utah, Montana, Missouri, Kansas, Louisiana, Mississippi, Indiana, Nebraska.

So currently a total of 18 states maximum, most with some cultural attractions and great cities; but also very limited overall economic impact on the country. If these States wish to continue following the lies of a wannabe white supremacist dictator and create their own country, in the end they really won't be missed. But the citizens of those States will suffer severe social and financial consequences.

The 32 remaining United States could quickly expand to 36 by adding D.C., Puerto Rico, the U.S. Virgin Islands, and Guam. Long overdue for all of them.

WHO WILL OBJECT:

Probably most red States currently on the cut line, and any lawmakers who could be facing sedition charges.

SOCIAL SECURITY

THE PROBLEM:

The threat being conveyed is that Social Security will run out of money soon and end, but the reality is quite different.

PRACTICAL SOLUTIONS:

Every year or so, maybe even every few months, dire warnings are circulated about the Social Security Trust Fund running out of money in a few short years, thereby lowering everyone's retirement benefits or perhaps eliminating them completely. This is what some propaganda peddlers want others to believe, but this nonsense will never amount to any substance of reality. Far too many people pay into the system, and far too many retirees depend on the system for their very existence, for it to ever fold up and go away.

In reality, it is an easy problem to solve.

In 2021, roughly 25% of all the expenditures in our country are for pension programs and Social Security. Less money may currently be coming in than is going out due to the fact Senior citizens are living longer now than ever before. That in itself is a good thing. But the solution is not to raise the FICA Social Security tax from its current 6.2% level. The answer is so much simpler than that.

Currently, wage earners do not have to pay the 6.2% Social Security tax on any income above $142,800. Why? It makes no real sense except to some politicians. After all, there is not an Income Cap on the Medicare tax, even if someone does not plan on ever using it. If you make ten million a year you still pay out 1.45% on it all. If the Income Cap for Social Security is removed completely the entire program will be funded in perpetuity, as in forever.

Will those making above the current level like the Income Cap being lifted? Probably not, but no one really wants to pay any taxes at all. They may claim they will never get a complete return on their investment. But should another Depression or Recession occur where they lose everything financially, where else will they turn? But read on into the chapter on Taxation, as people will no longer even see the 6.2% and 1.45% deducted from their paychecks.

Fully funding the Social Security Trust Fund will also allow for some very long overdue benefit increases, especially for Senior Citizens who are currently being funded well below the Federal Poverty Level for any number of unfair reasons. They definitely deserve better, and we must help rectify that sooner rather than later.

WHO WILL OBJECT:

Principally some of those making over the current limit.

SOCIAL SERVICES

THE PROBLEM:
The quality and availability of Social Services has been in decline and underfunded for far too long.

PRACTICAL SOLUTIONS:
With regard to those in American society who need the most help; the disabled, single mothers, the homeless, and others suffering from mental illness or drug/alcohol addiction there are potential cures, if leaders do their job to improve both urban and rural communities.

Back in the day when these services were provided by States and/or non-profit groups, essential services were readily available. When the private insurance industry bought out the healthcare marketplace and eliminated services in cost cutting moves, and when politicians decided they could no longer justify being able to afford to help others in need, it only exacerbated a growing problem.

Mental health facilities were shut down, public assistance community services curtailed, and disability rights overlooked for the most part. It resulted in an increase of homeless people through job loss and/or mental health and drug addiction. It led to people being denied basic necessary services such as mental health counseling, drug and alcohol addiction treatment; plus job opportunities, enhanced education, and affordable safe low income housing for anyone disabled or below the Federal Poverty Level.

There will always be a valid discussion and the related dichotomy about social welfare programs and their effectiveness, as well as the cost to society as a whole. Welfare is only supposed to act as temporary support until programs effectively put people back to work.

For anyone with children, whether single mothers, disabled or not, they will need pre-school child care help, low income housing allowances, food assistance, job opportunities, and counseling, to get them back on their feet.

But they must always show a willingness to actually improve their situation through this always very necessary but currently not totally available comprehensive help.

WHO WILL OBJECT:

Those who just see Social Services as being a handout being exploited by others.

SPACE EXPLORATION

THE PROBLEM:
Due to decades of inactivity, the world is catching up in the race to explore outer space.

PRACTICAL SOLUTIONS:
Private enterprise is better equipped to expand future ventures before other countries succeed in doing so. Delays in space travel progress are due to regulations placed upon NASA, an overpriced procurement system, and lack of expertise in Washington. Private enterprises function differently than government agencies, and are the future for all mankind.

In this century we will likely engage in extraterrestrial contact, as anyone who does not believe there is other life out there has to have blinders on, as it is a truly arrogant assumption we are the only beings in the vast universe.

Mining rich mineral deposits, finding new elements, perhaps developing colonies on the Moon and planets will be accomplished through technological and energy innovations far beyond what we could ever imagine. Future space discoveries will take us beyond any threshold we have ever experienced before.

WHO WILL OBJECT:
Those who feel space exploration or mining the future is somehow a huge waste of time and money.

SPORTS BUSINESS

THE PROBLEM:

Sports in America is a hallowed institution to some, but all the money involved leads to other concerns.

PRACTICAL SOLUTIONS:

It is telling that in a pandemic year where virtually no one was allowed to attend any sporting events in person, no sports teams went out of business and no players or coaches did not get paid. Other businesses folded and a lot of people lost their jobs or did not get paid, but college and professional sports teams got by reasonably well with no fans in the stands.

Obviously this is due to the enormous amounts of money television networks and other media platforms pour into collegiate and professional sports. The media needs programming so they can sell the expensive advertising which allows them to offer outrageous sums to schools and pro teams, which also contributes to the exorbitant salaries being paid to players and coaches alike.

Baseball is known as America's pastime and the average salary is now around $4 million a year, even if you're not really that good, just average. That's like $25,000 a game, even if you don't play. The minimum is close to $750,000, or about $5,000 a game; which is rather decent considering what most working Americans can ever hope to make in a year. In pro basketball the top players can make $250,000 or more per game, while the guys on the bench can still pull in over $10,000 a game. In pro football, the top guys can pull in at least $1 million per game, while the minimum players can still expect close to $30,000 a game.

Sure, some of these players may only be able to play a few years and should bring in as much as they can during the time they have; as injuries, declining performances, and salary cap casualties can and will cut careers short.

A lot of proponents who somehow can justify these salaries inevitably cite the entertainment value. But sadly, actual entertainers do not fail as much as professional sports players, or they would not even be professional entertainers much longer.

Sports do provide a world of hope for many underprivileged but talented players of many races to have a successful future. If you excel in high school there may be a college scholarship waiting, one that your family could not otherwise afford. If college goes well, even at league minimums, pro sports are a goldmine for these youths, and can lead to many other opportunities if they play their cards right. But since very few college athletes actually make the professional ranks, they must be counseled to utilize that college scholarship as an educational tool for their future.

On the other hand, professional sports have not been especially kind to women, or to players struggling in any of the minor sports leagues. Minor league baseball players, hoping to get ahead and being noticed, get paid very little and their living conditions are laughable, if not depressing.

Minor league basketball and football players are paid a pittance but just accept it in hope someone will notice their talents and invite them to try out at a higher level. It could be just a carrot and stick approach on behalf of those making the rules, but all these players could and should be making at least a livable wage for them and their families.

With women, where do we start about inequality? In pro soccer the issue of equal pay for both genders is still being argued even now, but since the women always outperform the men in international competition the subject should not even be debated. Let the women play in all the MLS stadiums and watch the seats fill up. In pro basketball the WNBA seems to continue growing in attendance and exposure, but player salaries lag far behind those of the men; whose owners control most of the women's pro league. The same inequality exists in golf, tennis, etc., where women continue to earn half or less of what men do.

In America we have antitrust laws which pertain to professional sports leagues like the NBA, NFL, NHL. But for some scurrilous reasons neither MLB or the NCAA are subject to these controls. Which begs the question of who is being paid off for this freedom not granted to any others? Old-timers spout baseball is a different story, but it is not.

As for the hallowed institution unto itself ruling most all college sports, having them subject to antitrust legislation will help eliminate some of its perceived abuses. This organization makes a lot of money for itself and member schools off of television and media contracts. Schools use this revenue to upgrade facilities, and give raises to those coaches and staff who have helped make it happen.

Who really loses out on this? Student athletes of course. Their athletic scholarships pay for tuition, room and board; but not all the other normal expenses incurred on a daily basis. Schools and organizations they are aligned with really do not want to share their revenue, but they could make a lot of student athletes very happy by even offering the Federal minimum wage for the time they are mandated to train and play, which non-athletes are not subject to. Schools and their representatives could easily work these cost increases into future media contracts with all the rival bidding companies. That is, if they really want to.

There is talk that the powers that be in college sports may be forced to allow athletes to sign lucrative Name Image Likeness contracts. Good for the big name football and basketball players, but bad for all other athletes in less popular sports who won't see a dime since Title IX probably won't be in effect.

Most Americans cannot afford to attend professional sports games unless their incomes are far above average. While not absorbing the whole fan experience, the game can actually be enjoyed and see it better from your couch. Even though teams still turn a profit when no one is allowed to watch in person, when full attendance is allowed fans still come regardless of how exorbitant the ticket prices are.

There is also the dangerous issue of legalized sports gambling, a very profitable venture for the betting houses, but just like casinos, the house was not built to lose. Only the bettors eventually do, and the fixes could be in.

WHO WILL OBJECT:

Some pro sports team owners, institutions, and their governing bodies. Student athletes will probably not object.

<u>SUBSIDIES</u>

THE PROBLEM:

Lawmakers in their zeal to allow more subsidies than which can be afforded.

PRACTICAL SOLUTIONS:

There is growing belief all subsidies except for low income housing and food should be eliminated from Federal budgets. This process cannot be decided by any Congressional body as they may have approved these subsidies for partisan or special interests in the first place.

There should not be any subsidies for any product unless adverse market conditions due to weather or disasters prove otherwise. American farmers and the crops and animals they produce will adjust, survive, and perhaps benefit on the free market if they are allowed to do so. If it doesn't work they will plant, grow, or nurture something else that will.

Subsidies are often handouts to rich corporations in control of small companies and farms. This must be eliminated as America is currently in a huge spending deficit hole which must be reversed for long term financial stability. Money that has to be borrowed from a foreign government is not a sustainable policy.

WHO WILL OBJECT:

Politicians and many receiving subsidies.

THE SUPREME COURT

THE PROBLEM:
Supreme Court Judges are political appointees who can serve for life. It has not ever been a good or fair idea.

PRACTICAL SOLUTIONS:
As supposedly the most hallowed judicial institution America has, and the ultimate final decree destination on the Constitutionality of any laws or suits presented before it, unfortunately this body fails as it is partisan aligned to those who placed them in what is currently a lifetime appointment.

Article II, Section 2, Clause 2 of the United States Constitution, known as the Appointments Clause, empowers the President to nominate, and with the confirmation of the United States Senate, to appoint public officials, including justices of the Supreme Court. The President has the plenary power to nominate, while the Senate possesses the plenary power to reject or confirm the nominee. But the Constitution sets no real qualifications for a Supreme Court Justice, thus a President may nominate anyone they wish, and if the Senate majority is aligned to the President, all they do is rubber stamp the nomination. The Founding Fathers may have expected more integrity from lawmakers, but this has not been the case.

Jurists of different political parties also have a serious dichotomy of interpretations in what Constitutional law should determine on any issue. Conservatives rarely agree with Liberals, and vice versa. It truly denigrates the authenticity of the Supreme Court as to the validity of its interpretations. Any decrees should not be one way or the other, as there is always an acceptable middle ground to explore. Otherwise it is just viewed as partisan politics at its very worst.

If the court must be expanded to an even number like 12 with an equal number of Liberals and Conservatives to make it fair no matter what party rules, then so be it.

Subsequently, those Judges who virtually accomplish nothing will be replaced through Term Limits, as it should be with all elected or appointed officials. 80 and 90 year old Jurists deciding contemporary issues for a younger, more progressive society is simply not good policy for the country.

As discussed under Judgeships, an independent body of legal professionals should approve or deny the choice of the Executive Branch, and no Senate Majority Leader should be allowed the power to stop any confirmation hearing from going forward for any reason whatsoever.

WHO WILL OBJECT:

The Executive Branch, the Senate, Political Parties, and all Federal Judges who feel they should be considered.

STATE'S RIGHTS

THE PROBLEM:
States should have more control over their land, but increased oversight with laws.

PRACTICAL SOLUTIONS:
The Government should empower all State's to have principal authority on issues such as Labor, Education, Commerce, Agriculture, Transportation, Energy, and Land use as it affects their state; all subject to prevailing laws.

But the Federal Government should hold presiding power over issues such as the death penalty, Federal Elections, and other Federal laws which extend over and above any old and oftentimes discriminatory State criminal laws.

Washington should let all the States fund everything else themselves. The best States will figure out how to do this by controlling their necessary expenditures without levying higher taxes, and by expanding business initiatives.

States that won't do this will probably lose residents who will choose to move to other more progressive states. Those State legislators responsible for the decline will inevitably be unceremoniously rewarded at the ballot box. That is exactly how the system should work.

WHO WILL OBJECT:
The States and Washington, but for various different reasons.

THE SUPERMAJORITY

THE PROBLEM:

The current 50+% Majority to pass a law is a joke.

PRACTICAL SOLUTIONS:

Nowadays, if either party controls either the Senate or House of Representatives, even by one measly vote, they can push through legislation that may negatively impact the other 49.9% of the non-ruling party. This is nowhere near a fair representation of all the people of the country, and it has led to disastrous partisan gridlock in Congress when true bi-partisan compromises are desperately needed.

Once the Electoral College is eliminated, so does the failed element of only having a two party political system. Maybe there is a Left Wing Party for true socialists and liberals, a Right Wing Party for true extremist right wing conservatives. But the rest of the moderates and progressives in both the Republican and Democratic parties may find themselves drawn to the middle or a Pragmatic/Progressive Party, which would likely be in the electorate majority. Parties with other agendas can also be included.

Like many other nations in the world, this can successfully lead to other political parties forming a different percentage of Congressional representation; and thus allowing a coalition government which truly promotes bi-partisan cooperation in bill passage, instead of the partisanship now dominating Congress inertia.

The absolute key to this bi-partisan cooperation is to not allow a slim 50.1% majority to legislatively determine anything for all the rest of us, regardless of our political persuasion. A 60% SuperMajority should be required to pass any legislation or to override a Presidential edit or veto as needed, and would also make bi-partisanship a requirement for legislators to stay in office. Because if those who are elected to Congress do nothing but object, for whatever reason during their term in office, they will probably be voted out of office during their next election cycle because they obviously didn't get anything meaningful done.

Term Limits and a fair SuperMajority consensus for Congress will both be progressive improvements and also speed up progress for our country in so many areas, rather than delay it as we can see it being done now.

WHO WILL OBJECT:

Congress, Republicans, Democrats, Lobbyists, PACs, SuperPacs, and Dark Money Devils.

FAIR TAXATION

THE PROBLEM:

The huge US tax code and its myriad deductions favor the wealthiest and is why some pay no taxes at all.

PRACTICAL SOLUTIONS:

The current unfair tax system in America is a true abomination, totally riddled with special interest provisions that are not for the benefit of lower and middle class workers, or the small companies that need it. It is set up to allow the rich to get even richer. That is why the wealthy enjoy so many deductions that the less fortunate financially cannot even use.

It may be how plutocratic societies such as ours see themselves flourishing, but history reminds us every empire set-up this way in the past has wound up crashing and burning to the ground. Not a very good course to follow.

To even the playing field, the answer is to institute a fair 20% Flat Tax for all Individuals, with no deductions other than that no one of any means would pay any taxes until their income passed a true Poverty Level Threshold for the size of their family. This is the one major key and only deduction necessary to achieving Fair Taxation. The only caveat is that this 20% tax also includes all the FICA taxes.

For Corporations and Businesses it would again be a flat 20% tax on any income, with absolutely no deductions allowed. Again, the caveat would be this would include FICA.

This is a fair system where no one is any longer punished for making more money, and also not rewarded for being able to utilize multiple politically instituted deductions to pay little or no taxes at all. It will actually generate much more revenue for the government, help spur the economy, and greatly increase the Gross Domestic Product.

The Self-Employed, for so long very unjustly taxed, would not pay a business tax, but they would still pay the Individual 20% tax, FICA included.

Integrating Flat Tax systems has been debated for many decades but never integrated due to politics. Proponents say it is fair to all and easy to regulate. Detractors claim a Flat tax will not raise enough revenue for the country to operate on. Actually it will create more revenue since the elimination of deductions will open up a vast new revenue source from profitable businesses and the very rich 1% of individuals, many of whom use a multitude of deductions to pay little or no taxes. How the Government chooses to spend that revenue is another matter entirely, and needless to say a definite concern.

Non-Profit Groups and Religious organizations would still pay no Corporate taxes as long as they could prove they were legitimately non-profit by spending not more than 20% of their total income for administrative costs, including all salaries. Otherwise they would be subject to the 20%

business tax. Even if they pay their leaders exorbitant amounts of money, all leaders and true salaried employees would still be subject to the 20% Individual tax, FICA included.

You may hear shouting and protests about this not being a fair solution to the taxation problem. From whom? Certainly not from Low Income people. Some in the Middle Class who are homeowners may legitimately cry about losing their Mortgage Interest tax deduction. Do renters receive any tax reduction on their housing? Not a cent.

People may question if this supposedly fair Flat Tax might somehow raise their taxes, but the take home pay for Individuals will actually increase by 7.65%, leaving an actual no deduction maximum tax rate of 12.35% for Businesses and Corporations. For the Self-Employed and Individuals it will actually be a little less since they won't be taxed on any income earned below the Federal Poverty Level.

Probably sounds pretty fair to most people. But some who are rich will cry at losing money through the loss of deductions they may have paid dearly to for lobbyists and politicians to push through. Some big corporations may essentially do the same, as they essentially object to paying taxes on any profits made. Sorry, but that game must end.

If we can control how much money is spent on bribing politicians through Campaign Contributions, Political Action Committees, and Lobbyists; then businesses and the wealthy will have little choice but to comply with the new tax formula. When they figure out how much they save by not employing a multitude of tax lawyers and accountants, their outlook may principally change.

Since this new tax system will also exponentially increase tax revenues from the rich, whether by Individuals or Corporations, as well as increase consumer spending; there is little to lose but also so much to gain. Putting more money into the hands of consumers every paycheck will greatly stimulate the economy as a whole. Plus, it will also help develop more small businesses in communities which desperately need such development; as well as making the reality of new factories and manufacturing enterprises much easier.

Tax revenue in America currently breaks down this way: Individual Income taxes amount for about 50%, Payroll taxes for 35% (which mostly gets funneled back into Social Security and Medicare), Corporate taxes only amount for a seemingly meager 9% (wonder why?), Excise taxes for 3%, and the remaining 3% for a combination of Customs Duties, Estate taxes, Gift taxes, etc.

What our Government actually spends its revenues on in relation to the Gross Domestic Product is another pertinent factor. About 25% is spent for Healthcare costs (principally Medicare and Medicaid), another 25% for Retirement (Pensions and Social Security), 12% on Military and Defense, 15% on Education, 5% on Welfare, and the remaining 18% is spent on Mandatory and Discretionary spending which can include Veterans Affairs, Transportation, Infrastructure, Interest on the National Debt, and many other things.

Enough money is already there for the Government to spend. How we control what they can spend is paramount for the financial success of this country. This new tax system will spur the economy to a higher GDP and more tax revenues from all sources, much more than ever before. The benefit to all of this is to create surpluses which will allow us to pay down the enormous Federal deficit that continues to sap our country financially. This is just common sense economics.

The most important question becomes how these lower taxes pay for all of what our citizens need? Simple, of that 20% total, 7.65% for Medicare and Social Security (with no income limits) and up to 12.35% for the Federal Government to fund both the Military and any remaining essential Federal Departments. With deductions eliminated and better financial management of the country's expenditures this will be more than enough to make our country stronger than ever before.

Take a look at how this 20% Flat Tax Solution will impact Individuals, Families, and Businesses.

Example #1: 1 person making $15,000 a year (which should be the new Federal Poverty Level for 1 person) = No income tax, but they would still qualify for full Healthcare & Retirement benefits (as they would under Medicare anyway). Any income above $15,000 for a single filer would be taxed at 20%, FICA included.

Example #2: A Family of 4 making $100,000 a year. The new Poverty level would now be $30,000 for this family ($15k+$5k+$5k+$5k), leaving a taxable income of $70,000 of which they pay $14,000 for an actual tax of 14%, which includes Healthcare and Social Security for the whole family. Net tax less FICA: 6.35%.

Example #3: A Family of 5 making 1,000,000 per year - $35,000 FPL=$965,000 taxable income. They would owe $193,000 or 19.3%, which pays for the families Healthcare and SS benefits. Net tax less FICA: 11.65%.

Example #4: 1 person making $10,000,000 per year -$15,000 PFL= $9,985,000. Total tax: $1,997,000 (19.97%), including FICA benefits. Net tax less FICA: 12.32%.

Example #5: A Business with $100,000 income = $20,000 tax (20%), FICA included. Net tax TBD, but could be as low as 12.35%. Not applicable to the Self-Employed.

Example #6: A Business with $1,000,000 income = $200,000 tax (20%), FICA included. Net tax TBD, but could be as low as 12.35%.

Example #7: A Business with $1 Billion income = $200,000,000 tax (20%), FICA included. Net tax TBD but could be as low as 12.35%.

Those who see these low figures may still argue that the rates are not nearly high enough to adequately support our Government's expenses. But with little or no deductions the revenue stream will actually surpass what the Government now receives, and it also lowers the tax burden for those who deserve it the most. If anyone tells you otherwise they haven't done their homework, or have other political biases.

One of the injustices in both the Corporate and Non-Profit/Religious systems has been the exorbitant salaries extended to CEOs and Church leaders. Under this system no matter how much any CEOs are overpaid, employees of corporations and churches will still give back at least 20% to the Government with FICA included. The only exception would be if they didn't keep their total administrative costs (including salaries) below 20%, in which case they would have to pay the normal business or corporate rate of 20%.

So what then would be the future of the IRS: With no refunds to process, there is just tax revenue to collect. With Individuals (including Self-Employed) this could be done on a monthly or quarterly basis, usually through payroll deduction. The same goes for Businesses and Corporations. Nonprofit and religious groups should be handled on a semi-annual or annual basis. The IRS can then focus its enforcement powers on any entity that does not truly report their taxes. The IRS will have fewer employees and a lower operating budget, but a broader emphasis on going after those they can prosecute for tax evasion. This will save the

Government more money than   is currently being prosecuted for collection.

WHO WILL OBJECT:

Corporations and individuals currently paying no taxes, the IRS, tax lawyers, accountants, some big churches, and members of Congress actively involved in tax deductions. Low and Middle income wage earners and their families, plus small business owners, will likely not object.

TECHNOLOGY

THE PROBLEM:
Is that there really isn't much of one.

PRACTICAL SOLUTIONS:
The success of our country as well the future of the rest of the world has always been fueled by technology whether it be by innovation, the modernization of laws, or pure unadulterated personal initiative.

This process has been bestowed upon humanity by a much higher power to help it evolve its natural development into future civilization. In all its areas whether it may be science, medicine, communications, energy, travel; the pursuit of technological breakthroughs should be honored, funded, rewarded, encouraged, and expanded so more great things will evidently come to pass for all of us now living. As well as for our children who will contribute to bring about the future in ways most of us can only even imagine.

In the 20th Century there was much learned we did not even foresee as even being possible. Automobiles, Televisions, Social Security, World Wars, Atomic Bombs, a Great Depression, Passenger Airplanes, Space Travel, Computers, the Internet, Cell Phones, Social Media, a viral Worldwide Pandemic, and so much more.

In the evolving 21st Century this miraculous trend will continue, and hopefully in ways we never thought were possible. In areas such as Energy, Communications, Science, Space Travel, and Medicine the future holds is wondrous potential. The realizations and creations to come from it will be almost unimaginable until they actually happen. All Electric airplanes? Wait for it, they are coming.

About this time one hundred years ago it was called the Roaring Twenties, a great advancement indeed from the past; but no one really had a clue as to what the rest of the century would bring. In our new Roaring Twenties we may see some of those amazing surprises very soon.

Sure, other countries will try long and hard to steal our ideas, just as we probably attempt to do with their ideas. It is now the way of the world thanks to internet access.

Here now, in 2021, people still do not know what to expect. But breakthroughs in many areas will bring a lot of miraculous things we will initially be amazed by, and then have these innovations just be part of our daily lives.

WHO WILL OBJECT:
Who will object to a brighter future?

<u>TERM LIMITS</u>

THE PROBLEM:
Term limits in government have been needed for a long time but those most affected by it do not want to let it happen.

PRACTICAL SOLUTIONS:
There should not be Lifetime Terms for anyone in any of the three Government branches, especially those politically appointed. Back in the day when our Founding Fathers wrote the Constitution, most people were lucky to live past the age of 50. With life expectancy now approaching 80, it is something they never could have foreseen happening nor incorporated into any discussions regarding Term Limits.

Our lawmakers are controlled by a lot of old Power Brokers in Congress and their Committees on Capitol Hill, some of whom may already be experiencing physical and mental incapacities and are clearly on the downside. Old age will always limit what any of us can do. Which few of those in power would ever publicly admit however.

Yet older, powerful, oftentimes angry Congressional Power Brokers still control much of what everyone else does, not only in Congressional chambers, but also for American citizens and the rest of the world as it relates to us. In other words, these dogs can't really hunt very well past their prime, but they still allow themselves to do so as it pays very well.

Most of these aging Power Brokers are not fueled with a clear vision of a future they cannot really foresee, but only by their desire to stay in power by using various often unsavory schemes to help keep themselves in office. Some older voters may actually prefer it that way, but younger more progressive voters definitely do not want grandmothers and grandfathers in their 70's to 90's; possibly in declining mental and physical health, to tell them what they can and should do to enhance either their present or their future.

The age of 75 should be the Maximum Retirement Age (MRA) for any Federal employee, including those in Congress, the Military, Supreme Court, and the Presidency. It will benefit the country in many positive ways. Age does not always enhance wisdom, no matter what those elders may claim.

If there are only two four year terms maximum for the President, all members of Congress should only be allowed a maximum of 16 years total, to allow for perhaps two different Presidential administrations. But only up until the age of 75. Federal Judges, including the Supreme Court, should also only get a maximum of 16 years in service, until age 75.

Could a House member run for a different office when their Term Limit is up? Of course. Become whatever the electorate decides for them. But only until age 75.

Another major benefit of Term Limits will also be to empower more younger, progressive thinking civil servants to step forward and help serve the country.

Since it can't be left up to the President or Congress to institute this very needed improvement which directly affects all of those people, Direct Democracy must inevitably come into play to correct this problem with a most needed Practical Solution.

WHO WILL OBJECT:

Members of the Military, Congress, Federal Judges, and others who are over 75 years of age or getting close.

VETERANS AFFAIRS

THE PROBLEM:

Veterans Administration is an agency nightmare to the detriment of those they serve.

PRACTICAL SOLUTIONS:

Most Veterans Affairs hospitals and facilities, due to their expensive and stifling political bureaucracy, and mostly outdated facilities and treatment programs clearly have not met the full needs of our mentally and physically disabled Veterans whom our country owes a great deal of debt to.

Keeping our Veterans on a diet of drugs does not really solve any of the patient's conditions. Making them wait to receive necessary or even life-saving treatment is an obvious and complete bureaucratic failure, and an ongoing nightmare for those who need help the most to survive.

It would be much better for these deserving patients to be incorporated into the current Medicare system where they would be able to receive better, faster treatment outside of the presently embarrassingly poor management dilemma drowning the current Veterans Administration system.

Every new Presidential Administration will promise to send in someone special with innovative ideas to change the operational culture, yet very few if any tangible results are ever really seen. Congress always promises to correct the ongoing problems but apparently does not have even the capability or actual intent to contribute anything meaningful.

The VA administration is a grave disappointment not only for Veterans but for our entire country as well. The best and most positive solution is to simply wipe the slate clean, and transfer Veterans into a more responsive and humane system with better and more progressive treatment.

We owe our Veterans a great deal, and they definitely deserve much more than they have been inadequately afforded so far. As with anyone experiencing medical or mental health issues, better comprehensive help, treatment, and compassion goes a long way towards achieving the goal of recovery.

WHO WILL OBJECT:

VA officials and the lawmakers overseeing thcm. The Veterans themselves will likely not object too much to the prospect of actually receiving better care.

WOMEN'S RIGHTS

THE PROBLEM:
Some women in America are still treated as second class citizens in both wage earning and value.

PRACTICAL SOLUTIONS:
The list is very long for Women's Rights. In America 100 years ago, the 19th Amendment to our Constitution finally gave women, who had definitely been around in America long before our Constitution was adopted, precisely 228 years, the actual right to even vote. Seriously? Yes. In some countries women still aren't allowed to vote.

Perhaps before then, Women were only seen as sexual or birth bearing companions, or perhaps the personal chattel of some kind. Men have had to slowfully and sometimes painfully learn how powerful Women actually are both emotionally and professionally. How they were treated in the past, and how they are still being treated in some ways now deserves much more than just anyone's apology.

About 70 years ago the United Nations enshrined that Women's Rights are fundamental Human Rights including the right to live free from violence, slavery, and discrimination. To be educated, to own property, to vote, and to earn a fair and equal wage. Some countries still do not allow much of this, as many Muslim countries continue to treat women as second class people, sometimes not even as citizens.

In America some but not all of those edicts have been followed, and those which have not been followed are the most worrisome. Equal pay for equal jobs still hasn't happened in the way it should have long ago. Both in business and in sports. Yes, there is talk it will happen, but still no resolution. Congress could change this, but if not, Direct Democracy can and will accomplish the right thing.

Better protection from domestic abuse, as in at least a DOJ Federal hotline, has not been a priority in what is still a very male dominated soceity. Reducing the horrible backlog of rape investigations and convictions continues to grow as it clearly seems as though many of the boys in charge would just like to look the other way by claiming they don't have the available manpower to do anything further or faster.

Guaranteed paid family leave from employers for Mothers of at least 16 weeks is not only fair but essential to keep making families strong. Even if this is offered at the prevailing unemployment rates, it is sadly not something the boys in charge are apt to embrace unless they are somehow forced to. Which can be done, and which has to be done.

Although more Women are running for public office and are logically winning many more elections through their promises for equality and often better organizational skills, even more determined involvement from women in all areas of Government is essentially needed to change the playing field. Some women who get elected may turn out to be crackpots, but the same holds true for men. They will lie and steal to gain power, much to the chagrin of the electorate who put them there. Depending on who they represent that can doom them politically.

America cannot any longer afford to continue to be a typical good old white boys club, and Women can help make it abundantly clear not only to other Women and Men, but most importantly to the young girls trying to wade through the ongoing male versus female discrimination; and the pretentious young male bullying towards perhaps extracting sexual submission from a young female desiring love and attention. Change the rules and you will definitely change how the game is being played.

Reauthorization of the Violence Against Women Act will definitely help, and also protection for immigrant Women. Rollback of Title 1X restraints on Women reporting sexual attacks in colleges is a necessity since many of these institutions seem more intent on trying to hide physical assaults in order to protect their reputations rather than protecting the victim's rights. Those schools allowing this injustice should be sued or prosecuted by whatever means necessary.

Women are a most valuable, equal, and essential part of our great society; far apart from their indelible affections and difficult but ultimately rewarding birth-giving capabilities.

Some men may be somewhat wary of Women who are not the submissive type, and also confused by any Woman's prerogative to disrupt affection or alliances based on whatever a Man feels he should have the right to be able to do at any given time. For men, it will always be a losing battle unless their priorities, integrity, and thought processes change.

Men should actually treat women exactly how they would wish to be treated themselves. It is called The Golden Rule. Ultimately, there is absolutely no real valid excuse in our minds or our hearts to not just do exactly that. It is long overdue.

WHO WILL OBJECT:
Whom might you think?

THE TRUE STATE OF AFFAIRS

So here we have now come to the end, or perhaps to the beginning, of what has hopefully been a comprehensive dissertation of ideas. Practical Solutions are very recognizable and can be presented in just a page or few. Why? Because the answers are relatively simple and easy to see for those who wish to see them. For those politically or financially affected by any change, that may well be a very different story.

Legitimately this discussion may be viewed as a new and necessary beginning for progressive thinking. There is no pretension here, unlike what many politicians try to portray to those whom they believe to be naive, that they can't ever truly understand any of these important subjects. But the truth is out there and is completely transparent. There are some who just don't want you to see how things really are.

There are no political or special interest precepts keeping any of us from looking for answers to our biggest and most serious problems in a world where we can either choose to be just a number in it, or be something much greater, and much more involved. In a very prominent way, as citizens of America it is our duty to do so. Speak up, ask for change, vote for it, then act for change if it doesn't happen.

We must implore ourselves and our elected leaders to adopt basic Common Sense in any decision making processes, as many of the problems we face have very Practical Solutions in how to solve them. If those in power actually desire to see them solved. Getting partisan bodies like Congress or even the Presidency to act progressively may ultimately be the hardest task, unless we utilize Direct Democracy to eventually change the ways in which our leaders allow themselves to operate.

Through the combination of National Referendums, Constitutional Amendments, and Direct Democracy a better will be created for us all. Once illicit money is no longer being funneled through to lawmakers from lobbyists and special interest groups, then the Federal Government will function more honestly and transparently. This will be to the benefit of America by eliminating the corruptive entities now controlling the system and eroding the integrity of many elected officials.

Demanding Criminal Justice reform, more domestic manufacturing jobs, a less expensive Health Care system, and a truly fair path to Immigration program, will all help pave the way to a brighter future. A crackdown on gangs, white supremacist groups, and other Domestic Terrorist plotters will help cleanse society of cancer caused by bigotry and hatred.

Combined with a truly Fair Flat Tax System, and by eliminating most of the unnecessary Subsidies being doled out; together this will help our country reduce the Federal Deficit, control budgetary expenses, and definitely make our country so much better for all of us to live and prosper in.

Evolution cannot really exist or progress anywhere in America or in the rest of the world without new ideas, the continual refinement of policies, and especially the bravery on the part of citizens to legally affect meaningful change.

These are some common sense Practical Solutions for America to adopt. For any truly Progressive thinkers looking ahead to the future and not wishing to delve back into all the sordid lessons of the past, these are sound modern ideas to help take both our country and all humanity forward once again; and hopefully in safe hands into the next century.

None of us of any political or religious persuasion can ever expect everyone to accept all the views which somehow do not mesh with their own. In truth, the world and all relationships in society would prove to be very boring indeed if everyone totally agreed on everything. We should never expect anyone else to always see things in the way we do. We can only hope they just might listen to a new idea.

What anyone of us ever chooses to believe in should not include hatred for anything or anyone we truly do not even understand. Diversity in ethnicity, skin color, and culture has always been the true color palette which has made America beautiful and strong. Hate is the only thing which can weaken the great promise for any country, and those who threaten this promise should be threatened themselves by laws to confine what must be construed as inherently evil ways.

Humanity not only embraces our power to discuss and reasonably resolve issues, but also helps us all manifest destiny in both the world and our very own fragile existence. One day or night we shall all inevitably die, but in the meantime there is so much more we can still do to greatly improve the lives of our parents, our children, and ourselves.

The secret to life has always been and will forever be just about loving, and the daily decisions we inevitably make along the way on whatever road we choose to follow.

THE END
(or perhaps a new beginning)

Necessary Measures

1. Prohibit convicted felons from holding office in the Federal Government, either through election or appointment.
2. Remove the cap on Social Security taxes to fund the program in perpetuity.
3. Increase the minimum Social Security payment to 110% of the Federal Poverty limit. Seniors shouldn't be in poverty.
4. Prohibit members of Congress, Federal Government, and Judiciary from trading stocks during their tenure.
5. Increase the Supreme Court to twelve members, 6 Conservative, 6 not, in order to finally ensure Bi-partisan decisions.
6. Impose 20% Flat Tax to all individuals and corporations.The only deduction is for the Federal Poverty limit.
7. Limit election campaign contributions to $25,000 for all individuals, businesses, and PACs to help ensure the rich cannot buy elections any longer.
8. Ensure that detained illegal immigrants are provided Due Process, and their whereabouts tracked.
9. Make attempts to bypass Constitutional laws by the President as grounds for immediate impeachment.
10. Make the Vice President an elected office rather than an appointment to ensure candidate qualifications.

11. Classify MAGA as the racist Domestic Terrorist Organization it clearly is.
12. Revoke pardons on all convicted January 6th rioters, even by charging them all with treason for their actions.
13. Restrict the President from revoking any Congressional approved funds, for any reason whatsoever, except a World War.
14. Institute Term Limits for all members of Congress, the Executive Branch, and the Judiciary; including the Supreme Court. No one over the age of 75 may serve.
15. Prohibit the President from deploying military units anywhere in the country, unless by a state's request.
16. Prohibit gerrymandering in all elections..
17. Institute the 60% SuperMajority rule in Congress to ensure equitable decisions.
18. Do not restrict abortions until the males involved are financially responsible.
19. Eliminate the Electoral College.
20. Overturn the Citizens United ruling.
21. Expand Medicare into Universal Health Care for everyone, including the Federal Government and the Military.
22. Tax churches like any non-profit group.
23. Remove any tariffs not approved by Congress on a SuperMajority vote.
24. End all non-humanitarian subsidies.
25. Provide more incentives for low income housing development.

AMERICA: PRACTICAL SOLUTIONS

AMERICA: PRACTICAL SOLUTIONS

STEVEN GRAHAM CHARLES was born in Northern California, the son of a portrait artist and a radio personality. He began writing early in life, but not until his young daughter Dyana asked what was happening in the bright stars above them one crystal clear night, did he start writing fiction. That is how **Stars In The Wind** began, circa 1975.

The author hopes his research driven non-fiction works will prove to be progressive, creative, and confrontational; such as political conflicts in the present world seem to demand.

America: Practical Solutions began in 2015 and evolved through world events and changing political perspectives. Critical current events have helped shape the final narrative.

The author's literary collection will be available through Amazon and Dancing Ground Entertainment.com for readers, bookstores, libraries, and film producers.

AMERICA: PRACTICAL SOLUTIONS